WE CAN SAVE THE WORLD

..but there's no money in it

PERI SCOTT

Affiliate disclosure:

As an Amazon affiliate I receive a small commission on sales generated by certain links in this book. I also may link to Apple Books as I am an affiliate with them as well.

❀ Created with Vellum

For my sons
May you change the world

INTRODUCTION

"It's hard to handle this fortune and fame,
Everybody's so different, I haven't changed"
"Life's Been Good" -Joe Walsh

Embedded within this 1978 classic by Joe Walsh are some themes that I could write a whole other book about. In fact; I must admit, I have spent considerable time "droning on" (as my kids say) about several of these themes in my blogs, articles, and the Scott family dinner table. What can I say? I like talking about money and classic rock.

One theme that pokes its head out of this lyrical masterpiece is that the singer has, what appears to be millions of dollars, but has no idea how much or what to spend it on. In fact, the comedic and sarcastic point of the song is to showcase just how much of an idiot you can be when you have money and no concept of its inner workings.

I have written books, articles and created online courses that teach people what to do with, how to make, invest, and budget money. I have worked really hard at advancing my own financial education by reading hundreds, if not thousands, of books on the subject. I have watched videos, attended seminars, and tried and failed in the real world of money. It has been a long and arduous journey with many roadblocks and disasters along the way, just to make it fun. I have been able to scrape together some good ideas and implement some strategies that have helped me and my family live a pretty good life, after starting out with very little.

In the process of learning how to "win" at the "game" of money, I learned the rules, figured out some winning strategies, and competed hard to get what I saw as my "fair share". It was a process that I had to initiate and pursue on my own accord. No-one was going to do it for me, and I had no-one to show me the way.

I often comment to my wife how weird it is that we don't know any rich people. We think about it and we tally up all of the people we know and almost all of them are pretty darn middle of the road on the economic scale. In fact we know far too many people who are living paycheque to paycheque and, sadly, we know more than one family that are near destitution. If we were to place our circle of friends and family on the global wealth scale, pretty much everybody we know are NOT in the fabled 1%. Not even close.

I started to really wonder why so many people are poor. In a world that has so many resources available and so much knowledge stockpiled in libraries, the internet and bookstores, how come everyone I know, including myself, are usually thrust into a life of constant struggle and strife. Why are most people forced to work at a job they hate, for barely enough money to get by for the next 30 days? We face 40 years of this "slavery" to finally collect a pension and retire when we are too old to enjoy it, hopefully slightly above the poverty line if we can swing it.

It made me start to think that the system might be broken.

I spent a long time figuring out how the system worked and how to use that to my advantage. I learned the rules and played the game to improve my station in life. I mastered some habits and shared my ideas with the world through my books. I thought that was the answer.

As much as I believed my work had helped people to improve their financial literacy and perhaps offer them a leg up, I still felt like I was trying to treat the symptoms instead of finding a cure.

This book is my exploration into the current capitalist system, and my attempt to find the nuts and bolts of its inner workings - and see if there really could be a "cure".

I have set out to explore capitalism and our economic model and see if I can understand the good, the bad, and the ugly, and perhaps indulge in some creative thinking along the way. I want to see if there is a way we can shine up the old jalopy and throw in a few customisations to make the most of it. Capitalism has been good to me and I feel like it has the potential to be good to all of us who choose to participate, if we learn how to use it properly.

I also want to take a little side trip into some alternative economic philosophies and shake up the old belief system. By contemplating ideas that might be outside of traditional thinking, I hope to highlight some important juxtapositions to traditional economic theory. We need to see the big picture and examine our way of life from a different perspective in order to put our current believe systems into the proper context. I will make the analogy many times in this book that "a fish doesn't know it is in water", because this exactly describes us. We are born into a society with customs, beliefs, rules, and paradigms that we accept as "normal" and oftentimes don't ever think to question them. We just accept things as "the way it is" and carry on with our lives, in spite of the fact that "the way it is" isn't really working...at least not for most people.

So, if you care to join me, I want to two-step into the world of money; and, more succinctly, ideas about money, and take a look around. Let's open up the hood and see if we can't tinker a bit to get a little more horsepower out of the old economic engine.

I think that ideas are the real catalyst for change in the world and my mission is to spread ideas. It is the first step in changing the world, as the invention of the printing press proved. If enough people learn about how our world works, and about the systems we are buying into, perhaps we can all participate in the gentle manipulation of our "beloved" system. We can change the world if we know what it is that needs to change.

Let's get started. Do not pass "Go"..

Chapter One

MONOPOLY

Monopoly is a very popular board game that has been around for generations, whereby families get together and try to financially ruin each other. One family member walks away rich while all the others wind up completely destitute - all in the name of good, clean fun. We think of this as a microcosm of the real world and we may even think that we are learning something about real estate investing.

Like many games, the objective is to win. There are winners and losers and this concept generally reflects life as we know it. I know I have heard the following:

"It is a dog-eat-dog world and the sooner you accept that, the better off you will be. "

"Everybody is out to get you"

"Make sure you are not being a sucker."

"It's not personal, it's business." - (You can make some very horrible decisions when you learn to compartmentalise these two things - as gangster movies have demonstrated).

Why do we have these ideas in our mind? They don't make me feel very good inside when I contemplate them. I like playing monopoly, because it is just a game, but playing the game of life with the same mindset may not be the right approach.

The origins of the game of monopoly are very interesting to me.

The well-known version of the story is that a man named Charles Darrow created Monopoly sometime in the 1930s, during the great depression. He sold it to Parker Brothers and went from rags-to-riches, igniting the hopes and dreams of many Americans that overnight success was not only possible, but probable via the principles taught in the game. The rules were a microcosm of the real world, where fortunes were made and lost via shrewd "gameplay" and wheeling and dealing.

The lesser known, more true-ish story is that Darrow may have "borrowed" the idea from a game called "The Landlords Game" - published decades earlier by a formidable woman named Elizabeth Magie.

Magie was a woman who was ahead of her time. She was one of the first true feminists, and created a lot of controversy through her exploits. She was self-sufficient, not marrying until she was in her forties. She spoke out against the treatment of women, even taking out an ad in the newspaper offering herself for sale as a "young woman American slave" to the highest bidder. She was trying to make women be seen a people, not possessions - a very controversial point of view at the time. A woman's perspective on economics was not very welcome in those days either - yet we will see later that her ideas were not only far ahead of their time, they were possibly the missing piece of the puzzle that our modern world needs.

Her game, "The Landlords Game" was also meant as a teaching tool. It had two sets of rules you could play by, and each had very different objectives and outcomes.

Just like Monopoly, there was a set of rules whereby one person would end up with all the money and everyone else was eliminated from the game. This is the version that caught on, and became popular. The other set of rules made it possible for everyone to benefit from any wealth that was created. People wondered what the point of that was.

It appears that her political beliefs about monopolists were reflected in her board-game, and she was well known for trying to get people to see the world differently.

She believed that the "alternate version" where everyone could benefit from wealth creation was a matter of morality. She believed that the pursuit of wealth for oneself and building a fortune on the backs of the poor was somehow linked to one's propensity for good and evil.

Perhaps.

I think she had a concept in her mind that has been better defined by modern thinkers but she just didn't know how to frame it properly. It is a concept that was not yet fully formed due to the pervasive nature of the paradigm she was fighting against at the time. I applaud her convictions. It is not surprising that Darrow made millions from monopoly and it is reported that Ms. Magie made around $500 from her version in the end.

Is there a different way to think? Monopoly tried to teach us a lesson. That lesson, it has been suggested, is that eventually, if we keep playing the "game", then eventually one person will win and get all the wealth. That sounds like fun for the winner but not so much for everyone else.

Is that the only way to play? Maybe there is another idea?

I recently learned a card game called "Hanabi". Have you ever played it? The first time I played, I was a little confused.

"How do I win at this?", I asked, as did everyone else at the table.

Actually the point is simple. Try to make *everyone* win. If you fail, then everyone loses. It was a severe departure from what I was used to. How did one go about doing that? It is really fun, and the strategy involves trying to help each other by communicating, via your choice of card, and trying to read other players' intentions. It is fascinating, challenging and surprisingly satisfying when you succeed.

I found it amazing that it is so popular. My favourite thing about Hanabi is the reaction of some people when it is brought out on game night. They ask "what are the rules?". We say,"to help everyone win!", and people look confused and resist. They say they don't want to play if they can't win.

WOW! How we have been indoctrinated. I wonder if we are that way naturally or if it is learned behaviour. If we look at every component of the world through the exact same lens all of the time, we tend to limit our options. Like the old saying "A hammer thinks everything is a nail" - a person who approaches every situation as a competition will often times not realise there are other approaches that would have a different outcome - perhaps the greater good would be served, or everyone would prosper (including yourself).

Not really something that is apparent at first.

Instead of a foray into nature vs. nurture and how psychologists have determined whether or not this is normal behaviour, I would rather look at other reasons that may have caused this attitude to be so prevalent in our society. Why is it that we tend to believe that there needs to be a winner and a loser in every transaction?

One theory is that we have lived in a patriarchal, male-dominated world for a long time.

It comes as no surprise that a new perspective on how to play the "Game" was invented by a woman who was also interested in feminism and equality. She understood that sometimes you play to win, and sometimes you play for the good of everyone. We will talk about this later.

If Ms. Magie had lived to see where we are today, I think she would be equally impressed that we have considered her ideas and fully extrapolated them into workable philosophies; and, disappointed that it has taken so long.

Monopoly was design to show us the problems with unabated capitalism, not to celebrate it. Yet, it is often our children's first taste of how money and assets work. This is a little sad; however, I don't blame people for not being aware of this. Our economic system has been one particular way for along time, and it is not about to change overnight. That is OK. We just need to keep planting the seeds of change.

Chapter Two

THE MONEY MINDSET

Win or lose

We understand this idea. We compete and then there is a winner and a loser.

Simple.

Everyone agrees on the rules and we celebrate the winner and the loser is forgotten. The loser can just suck it up. That's life.

The idea that there always has to be a winner and a loser seems very simplistic when you look at it from the outside. When you realise that there is another way to think, you begin to see "normal" human behaviours and concepts in a whole new light. It starts to make less sense than it did before. We wonder why we are often called sheeple as we just follow the rules and forget that we made the rules.

The old tradition of the divine right of kings is a perfect example of this. People believed that the monarchy were people that were ordained by God to rule over the common people and were basically without any sort of accountability to anyone but "God". This sort of system can only work if everyone agrees to it. The people born into this system may not ever realise that there is another system (ie. democracy) that everyone could agree to. They just blindly think "This is the way it is" and carry on with their life. Only when the current system becomes unbearable or wildly oppressive do they start to wonder if there is a better way.

We forget that every person is just a plain-old person. We are all equal. We are all sovereign beings that are equal parts of the whole of humanity. It is only through our "ideas" that we start to give others power over us. No one is truly more important than we are, or really has the right to decide our fate, unless we give them that power. Laws, countries and hierarchies are something we are familiar with that make us feel "safe" (sometimes), but they are not immutable laws of nature. They are human constructs. We just all agreed to abide by them. If we collectively decided to do something different, then we would be free to do so.

The funny thing about what I just said is that it is considered heresy or illegal in some places. It may even be considered crazy or anarchistic in other circles. I am just deconstructing sociological ideas into their base elements, yet certain people tend to place SO MUCH weight onto these ideals and ideologies, that some would murder me and feel justified about it if it conflicted with their ideas. I am suggesting that we can decide to do things in a different way than they have "always been done", and hopefully that new way would be a slight improvement over the way it was.

There has been amazing progress made in the sciences of sociology, psychology and the various permutations of these disciplines. Studies have been done on almost every aspect of human behaviour, and the conclusions sometimes are far from what we would expect. One example of this is a book I recently read called "friend and foe".

This book is an examination of cooperation vs. competition, and shows how each approach has differing level of effectiveness depending on the situation. Sometimes cooperation is called for, and sometimes competition is more appropriate. One of the book's main ideas is that neither philosophy is "better" or "worse" than the other, they are actually complimentary and are just tools in the toolbox to be used in the right situations. Like I said before, "A hammer thinks everything is a nail" is not very useful and this applies to economics as much as any other aspect of human existence. I will discuss this book in greater detail later, but a wonderful predecessor to this idea is the work of Riane Eisler.

DOMINATION MODEL

After reading "The Real Wealth of Nations" by Riane Eisler, I think the ideas I had been talking about in my previous books finally came into focus. I had previously been talking about a concept I called "Tempered Capitalism", and Cooperation vs. Competition for a long time, but Ms. Eisler did the hard work of thinking about these concepts thoroughly enough to find a possible root concept. She may have identified the genesis of the world paradigm we all believe is "The way it is".

She labels the historical mindset we have lived by for centuries as "Dominance" or more specifically "Male Dominance". Being a very prominent and respected feminist, she views the planet's ills as being a result of a male-dominated culture. She suggests that the idea of dominance or "survival of the fittest" is a predominantly male trait, and cooperation or **caring** is a predominately female trait. Because the world has been ruled by men for so long and women had been relegated to lower status (sometimes even being considered "Property"), we have made many other sociological constructs very male oriented as well. We tend to conceptualise the inner workings of our society in a dominator, or male way. We accept that business is "dog eat dog" and there is always a winner and a loser. We accept that 80% of the money in the world is owned by 1% of the people; we believe that that is just how it works. We may even hate it and protest against it in some sort of "Occupy" movement, but we don't know what else to do about it because it has been that way for such a long time.

Ms. Eisler takes current economic theory and frames it against a patriarchal paradigm and it tends to fit quite nicely. She made me realise that we are placing value on the wrong things.

She evangelises an economic model that places male and female traits and ideals in a balanced, equitable partnership. She does not believe that females or cooperation should now rule the world, she believes that there is a necessity to have equal importance given to each.

COOPERATION VS. COMPETITION

I first became aware of the study of these concepts when Malcom Gladwell wrote about cooperation vs. competition in his book "Outliers". It was quite a shock to many people when he presented scientific studies that proved cooperation was far more effective in many contexts than competition. Even in the world of sports, he gave examples where teamwork triumphed over individual efforts. I believe this was eye opening for many people when he first suggested it, yet he didn't even take it as far as he could have. It is, once again, not suggesting that one is better than the other, it is suggesting that both have a very important place in our world, and it may be high time to stop believing that dominance or competition is the only way to go.

Like Mr. Gladwell, Galinsky and Schweitzer, and Ms. Eisler all suggest, there is a place for both competition and cooperation in our world. We just need to use them in the right context and with the right checks and balances. Sometimes aggression is called for, sometimes negotiation and discussion. One cannot be subservient to the other.

Charles Darwin is often mis-represented when people say "Survival of the fittest". This does not mean survival of the strongest or toughest or most aggressive. Darwin actually postulated that it is more along the lines of "survival of the most adaptable". The species that can adapt to changes in their environment are the most likely to survive. This is very relevant to our world today. I take this to mean that the most adaptable are those who can switch from competition to cooperation and back again depending on their circumstances. Our world is changing too fast to be stuck in one modality or the other.

They say that "the only thing that is constant in our word is change", and that has never been more true than today. Our world is changing at a rapid rate, and not only in a technological sense. Even our culture and ideas are changing faster than a lot of people are comfortable with.

So maybe it is time to stop reacting to change and start initiating change. We need to understand that we are the change makers.

The #metoo movement has been a spectacular example of an awakening to the male dominated thinking that we have been accustomed to. It is a reaction to a practice that previously was "just the way it is" or "a harsh reality" that was "part of the business" where men could behave like jerks and women just had to grin and bear it. Who in their right mind would allow such a system to continue for so long?

Now the danger here is that men, in an effort to respect and understand the plight of their female counterparts, become a little too sensitive, caring and cooperative. They may lose sight of their inherent masculinity. Masculinity has been villainized due to the unfair advantage of being male in the past. The trick is to not throw out the baby with the bathwater. Men and women are different and that is a beautiful thing. Masculinity and femininity are both necessary and vital components of humanity, so to emasculate men to compensate for male dominance in the past is not a solution. Neither men nor women would benefit from this. Let us strive for "Not better than, but equal to".

MEN

Why would men think misogyny was OK? Because they were in charge. If you were a man, and in a powerful position, it was an unspoken rule that you can have anything you wanted, whether it was illegal, immoral or otherwise. The world worked that way for centuries, maybe even millennia, so who would willingly want to relinquish that kind of power? If I really think about it, why would men of that generation even have a reason to question the behaviour? Patriarchal dominance is like many of the concepts in this book, it's been "the way it is" for so long, it's never occurred to anyone to believe it could, or even should, be different. That is the problem with "beliefs". We don't question them, because we believe them to be true. Why would you wonder whether or not something were true if you believed it were already true? There is the paradox. This is the problem with systems that are broken. They are often not examined through a critical lens until they reach a breaking point. The world, being designed for the benefit of men, was not a conscious decision made by any one person at any one particular moment. It was a culture refined and repeated over centuries. And if the people in power were the ones to make the change, it really didn't seem to benefit them to change it. Once again, it didn't occur to them.

The concept of a partnership between men and women, a symbiosis of yin and yang is proven to be a much better way to operate in the world. But remember the saying about the hammer and nail. A male, competition-centric approach was really the only strategy that occurred to anyone at the time, because that was the paradigm. It would have seemed silly to compete against a woman, because they are meek and physically smaller than men. It would have seemed ridiculous to have expected them to have any status as they couldn't fight.

See the problem? Fighting (a male trait) was the only response to every situation, because men were the ones dictating how everything was done. The competitive, posturing approach permeated into every aspect of modern life, including the nuclear family, business, economics, politics, and social behaviour. Anything non-manly was ridiculed and devalued.

Now I am not saying that men are inherently immoral or evil. That is ridiculous. Most men are pretty decent human beings as are most women. But as a fish is unaware that it is in water, if you live in a world where men behave "this way" and women are treated "that way", you may not realise that these ideas are not actually right, even if they may "feel" wrong from time to time. You accept that it is just the way it is, because you have nothing to contrast it with.

I am an optimist. I think we humans, as a species, are destined for greatness. We just need to trip over ourselves a few times as we progress. It is going to be ugly and awkward as we make our way forward. We are going to regress, because it feels "safe" to fall back into our old ways. We are not going to go into a new world in a straight line, but I believe it is inevitable that we will become our best selves eventually.

Riane Eisler proposes a model of the same ilk. Dominance being replaced with partnership. Perhaps she has a better handle on the concept of cooperation vs. competition than I do; however, her observations paint a slightly more sinister picture than mine. I believe that most men are genuinely OK with a partnership model of the world these days.

Simon Sinek mentioned, in an interview with Marie Forneo, that fundamentally, whether people choose to cooperate or compete is largely determined by how safe they feel. If they feel safe and cared for in a particular environment, they will naturally cooperate and support others; whereas, in an environment where they feel unsafe or threatened in any way, they will naturally look out for #1 and do anything they can to survive. This can be extrapolated out to any scale, and it appears to be the case most of the time.

If we look at people who are living in poverty they tend to not feel "safe" in several respects, including, but not limited to:

Worrying how to pay the rent

Worrying how to eat

Worrying how to keep the electricity on

Worrying how to retire

Worrying about walking to school.

Worrying about the next guy getting his piece of the pie and you getting nothing.

Often, poverty determines where you can afford to live and it unfortunately places people in neighbourhoods that are unsafe - as the cycle of poverty creates many other societal problems like crime, substance abuse, and violence. This becomes another example whereby there is very little chance of escape, as there is nothing nearby to contrast this state of being with. This is the impetus for mixed demographics being part of good urban planning. I will talk much more about that later.

If we collectively decided that making people feel safe was a priority, it would have repercussions on many of the other issues we deal with. This would be a great example of a caring economy, and it would go a long way to solving many problems that society spends time and resources to fix from a reactive stance.

Without having to deal with the symptoms of poverty, let us deal with the root causes. Let's take a proactive approach to dealing with poverty. Let's start by caring about it.

Riane Eisler makes a very strong argument that the solution to economic disparity is to place more value on the things that actually matter. She called this a "caring economy".

One great example she offers is child care. If you really think about it, all the aspects of birthing, taking care of, and teaching a child are probably the most important things a person can do. The job of actually making a person, and ensuring that they are healthy, happy and well adjusted enough to make a positive contribution to the world can not be understated. I really can't think of any activity that has more of an impact on whether we move forward as a species or not than making people. Yet we consider child rearing to be a low value activity.

I won't go into it here, but Ms. Eisler speaks to the actual economic benefits of a caring economy where we value life, the environment, and the greater good. She actually shows the math. It makes sense. We would all prosper if we just made the right things matter.

So even if you are not a "touchy-feely" type of person, it is hard to argue with actual hard facts. She shows the economic benefits of placing appropriate value on things and activities that previously were considered the realm of "hippies" and "the weaker sex".

So where do we begin?

What does a world where we work together in partnership look like?

We will examine a few ideas next.

Chapter Three

PHILOSOPHY OF MONEY

What do we want?

How much stuff do we need?

If we truly wanted to think globally and try to benefit humanity as a whole we just need to take a critical look at the world of retail markets. If I go to my local shopping mall and try to buy shoes, I am usually overwhelmed by the sheer volume of the choices before me. There are so many shoes. So many styles, and colours, and brand names and it seems to be infinite. Some would say, "awesome". Some might say, "Why do we need so many shoes?"

Wouldn't it behove us, as a species, to make just enough shoes so that everyone had a pair, and then stop making so many more? Make them well enough so that when they eventually wear out, you can get another pair. Hey, let's go crazy and make a couple of styles so that you can mix and match. The problem is, there are probably enough shoes being made that it exceeds the number of feet in world by a factor of 10 - yet many people in the world go without shoes. How many shoes do we really need?

This is an extreme example to make a point. In an economy that is biased towards competition, two or more shoe companies will create a bunch of shoes with the objective of selling more shoes than the other guy, instead of just making enough shoes so everyone can have a pair. There ends up being twice as many shoes as there needs to be. The resources that went into making all those shoes to win a "game" were put towards an end that serves no greater purpose than to make one company richer than the other.

The same can be said about many products out in the world. I love that we have choice. I love that competition inspires innovation and progress. But should that be the only goal? Should there not be checks and balances built into the system to keep capitalism from running amok? Profit at any cost?

The original model of economics was traditional based on trade. Then it evolved over time to include lending or debt. This of course led to usury and corruption. Our current economic system is built upon debt. The original treatise on modern economics was "The Wealth of Nations" by Adam Smith. He conceptualised a great many economic fundamentals and we still adhere to many of these principals today.

Economics took a nasty turn in the 20th century when a brilliant economist name Milton Friedman made the notion popular that the only purpose for a company was to benefit its shareholders. In spite of this man's other very progressive and interesting works, this one particular notion opened the door to corporate madness. It became a common idea that profit at any cost was OK and morality became second. Companies did unethical and illegal things just to make a profit and increase share valuations. It was a slippery slope that has resulted in many public humiliations and failures by previously respected companies.

But times are changing. Many companies are starting to recognise that this policy is not sustainable. The world has a way of reminding us that long-term thinking is usually the best policy. Nothing happens in a bubble. We are all connected.

Patagonia recently took out an ad in the NY Times and declared "Do not buy this jacket" - referring to a jacket that they, themselves, manufactured and sold. In the ad, they detailed the resources that were consumed to produce the jacket and the resources it took to distribute and sell it. They pointed out that the jacket left behind two-thirds its weight in waste and pollution to get it to market. The message was "only purchase stuff that you need".

Wow.

Imagine if every company had this approach. The world would be very different. We would consume a lot less and maybe we would stop equating happiness with things. Maybe we would spend more time with family and friends and valuing people and shared experiences instead of the bottom line. Maybe we would take the time to work on ourselves.

It may seem like a fantasy world where this ad could have actually happened. Many people more cynical than I would chalk this up to a publicity stunt. I don't care. Even if efforts to move the world towards a new paradigm of caring and responsibility are just lip service to boost sales, I am still ok with it. The ideas must be spread. This stuff is happening right now in the real world. People are waking up to other ways of thinking and it is awesome.

Douglas Kruger says "To solve poverty, raise excellent human beings." This is a very successful money mentor giving advice to those that struggle financially. It is not "Do whatever it takes to make a quick buck". It is a very profound statement that has real long lasting positive effects. This advice is not offered lightly. Those that have achieved financial abundance tend to offer advice contrary to what many people expect. Poor people have some strange beliefs about what is required to become wealthy and then they wonder why they stay poor. Listen to the wealthy, they know what they are talking about.

Jordan B. Peterson believes that the way out of what he calls "tribalism" is to elevate the individual.

> *"Being the best version of yourself encourages self efficacy, self reliance, critical thinking and a healthy assessment of where we fit in the world. If we "figure ourselves out" we are less likely to succumb to group thinking and conforming to the crowd. We are less likely to be led astray by a charismatic leader bent on destructive agendas. By being strong individuals we can organise and create new ideas and policies that benefit everyone and overcome some of the old ways of thinking. The uneducated and narrow minded tend to resist change, even if it is for the better, because it is more comfortable to do "what you know" than to go into the abyss of the unfamiliar. "*
>
> — 12 RULES FOR LIFE - JORDAN PETERSON

Which leads me to another concept that is similar and just as terrible.

The instant gratification principle.

I have written about this many times before in my books and my blog and here I go ranting again. But I have to. Part of what makes our modern world so wonderful and terrible all at the same time is the fact that we have the ability - the sheer technological and intellectual ability to ensure the health and well being of every person on the planet - yet we don't.

Why not?

Because there is no money in it. That is part of the problem - we live in an instant world where a short-sighted idea like this actually makes some sort of diabolical sense.

We want everything right now. We get fast food and on-demand movies. We want a pill to help us lose weight and a million other things that used to take time and effort to acquire are now instantly available. This instant access tends to lead us to believe that absolutely everything should be instant - including solutions to our big problems.

I understand this thinking to an extent. Because we live in a capitalist society where money basically equates to "LIFE" it becomes a matter of life and death pretty quickly. We need money to live. We need money to eat, to put a roof over our heads and to stay warm. Our quality of life is determined by how much money we have. They are inextricably linked as far as we can tell. Our "success" in life is measured by our net worth. You would be hard-pressed to find many people who would disagree with this notion. So when you have an idea in your head that your "life" is in jeopardy for any reason, you will make a decision that will bring you back to the feeling of "safety" no matter how short-sighted it is in the grand scheme of things. However understandable this behaviour is, it is a flawed perspective.

The solutions to hunger, and poverty and overpopulation are not going to be instant or easy or simple. They are going to take a long time, require hard thinking and the will to overcome the hardest obstacle of all, the status quo. People are afraid and resistant to change. They are all thinking in the limited way that "if one person get something, that leaves a little less for me."

WINNERS AND LOSERS

We accept that the people who have it the toughest in the world just simply fall into the "loser" category and that is that. No need to really care. Some bleeding heart actor who is desperate to revitalise their popularity is going to go make a big deal about it and all will be good.

This is not the case. We need to fundamentally change our perception of each other, and in turn, our economic paradigm.

We need to start caring about the right things. Our economy is based on giving a monetary valuation on things- and we tend to value male things over female things. One glaring example is how much money is spent on the military, especially in the USA. Not that the military is unimportant. Once again, the goal here isn't to have one side win and the other side lose. The goal is to put a proportionate value on each.

> *"According to World Military & Social Expenditures, the cost of a U.S. intercontinental ballistic missile would feed 50 million children, build 160,000 schools, or open 340,000 health centres. According to a UNICEF report, the cost of one nuclear submarine would provide low-cost rural water and sanitation facilities for 48 million people, and the cost of eleven radar-evading bombers could provide four years of primary education for 135 million children"*
>
> — THE REAL WEALTH OF NATIONS - RIANE EISLER

So the problem here is not that competition is "bad". It is a real thing. But it is not the ONLY thing. Competition has its place in human interactions, but it needs to be knocked down a peg or two and relegated to a tool in the toolbox, rather than the bedrock for all human interactions.

So our ideas about money are fundamentally askew. We rely on the advice of people who themselves are not rich. We watch TV and movies depicting overnight success and impossible dreams becoming reality in a 2 minute "training montage". We believe that if we can't become rich quickly, it isn't worth getting rich at all.

This is all silly.

Chapter Four

NEW IDEAS

OK smart guy. What is the plan? How are you going to change the world?

Well, I am pretty sure I am not the guy to ask. I will leave that planning to the really smart people out there, who have spent a large portion of their lives thinking about these things and have offered up some pretty good ideas. I am just putting forth a few of them here in one place for your consideration. I am not going to say any one of them is the golden ticket, I am just saying these are a good start to get us thinking about possible ways to improve the inherent flaws in the current system.

UBUNTU CONTRIBUTIONISM

I read a book entitled Ubuntu Contributionism by Micheal Tellinger. In it, he spends an equal amount of time lambasting capitalism and the giant global conspiracy that is the foundation of our economic system, and a new economic model based on an ancient African philosophy called "Ubuntu". He also took some time to offer up some possible solutions to our current state of affairs.

The solution is to de-centralise the power systems, by reverting to "tribal" type living. He suggests we move out of cities and revert to small, self-sustaining communities that try to adopt a hybrid economic model where everyone has a profession that suits them, makes them happy, and provides value to the community. A council of elders make the decisions and each community needs all citizens to contribute to the greater good in equal amounts. The model works on an honour system, where everyone in the community contributes time each week to community works, in whatever form they can provide, depending on their abilities and expertise, then the rest of the time they are free to do as they wish.

His math argues that in most scenarios the average person should only have to contribute 4 hours per week in order to maintain the sustainability of the community. All community projects are voted upon and worked on by the community as a whole. That free labour translates into all being fed, sheltered and clothed, at a minimum. After that, you are free to pursue your heart's desires. Professions such as medicine and law will once again be pursued as a "calling" instead of just a lucrative career path.

It sounds a bit like communism, yet it has a different vibe to it. He is talking about valuing the community and the well being of everyone above that of the individual. He puts elders in place to make decisions instead of politicians. He stumbles into the philosophy of cooperation instead of competition without realising or articulating it, yet it is the underlying foundation of the philosophy.

If we compare this idea to those of Riane Eisler, we see that he was on the right rack, but hadn't fully figured out the base philosophical foundation that the system would build upon. The dominance mindset of traditional thinking is what he is fighting against in his tirades against the "man" yet he doesn't appear to quite know it. His idea of a community based society is parallel to the cooperation or partnership idea. If we truly understand that cooperation is necessary, and further understand how the dominance model is failing us, we can conceive that the partnership model is the template for a new system and the building blocks of an actual workable Ubuntu Contributionism are there. We can now take a half-baked idea and transmute it into a fully formed economic system, because we will understand what the parts represent. Each "corrupt" or "Immoral" component of the old economic system can be seen through the lense of "Dominance" and understood for what it is, and why it is, and where it came from. It no longer feels like a conspiracy theory, it becomes more like a failure to realise we are fish in water. Each "cool idea" or Ubuntu community systemic component can be filtered through the lens of "partnership", blending the male and female, and the right tool from the toolbox to the right job. This can be a far more succinct and well-formed model, when we understand the genesis of both the problem and the solution.

CONTRIBUTION

timebanks.org is a website that offers up "credits" for doing good works or community minded activities. This encouraged people to contribute to society without expectation of anything intern other than to make the world abetted place. It is similar to the Ubuntu model and could be expanded to just about anything we want. Imagine if all civil activities were done voluntarily - imagine if we truly valued the world we live in at several levels. We value our home and our family and voluntarily contribute our time and talents to making those things better. Then we value our community and offer our time and talent to help that flourish. We value our society as a whole and on and on until we value the earth. We contribute some of our time and talent to the health and well-being of the planet as a whole. Even to humanity as a whole. I would love to see the math there, how much time would it take each of us to collectivity make a difference to all those different levels. I imagine it not only needs to be a matter of philosophical change, but behavioural changes as well. Processes and procedures can only do so much, we need people to think differently too.

If we have and economic system that values things such as family, community, environmental sustainability, and preservation of life, then the right actions will appear. We will measure our success as human beings and countries and corporations by these new markers, not GDP and share valuation. We can save the world, and there may even be money in it after all.

Now in looking at Ubuntu Contributionism, it is apparent that it is a very socialist point of view. It seems to be very much in line with "Collectivism" and it makes sense from that perspective. But it is not balanced. If you read the book, it suggests that each community still has a "trade" or product/service that they offer to the world in exchange for money, but I would argue that the scales are definitely tipped towards the benefit of the whole, not the individual. This is why it probably will never see the light of day, and wouldn't work if it did. We cannot disregard human ambition and self service. People are driven to their own betterment as much or if not more than towards the greater good. This is human nature. It is a wise, self-aware individual that can see the big picture and integrate the whole of humanity or even his local tribe into his everyday concerns and activities. We should strive to implant this idea into our heads without removing the necessary mechanisms that drive ambition. We need to always be striving for a balance between the two ideas. Collectivist ideas must be tempered with Capitalist ideas in order to preserve our humanity. Capitalism has given so much, yet it is not perfect and we cannot ignore the problems that have arisen because of its unencumbered rampage. But the solution is not to go to the extremes of the other end of the spectrum and only think about our collective well-being. That creates indifference and stifles creativity. There is a symbiotic relationship to be had between the individual and the whole. Capitalism and collectivism are two equal parts of a healthy economy and essential pieces to our collective psyche. We must learn to embrace, respect and utilise each philosophy in the proper contexts. We will destroy ourselves if we cannot find that equilibrium.

Chapter Five

UNIVERSAL BASIC INCOME

Universal Basic Income (UBI) is an idea whereby the government (or some other benevolent governing body) distributes a sum of money to every single adult person in a society without any strings attached. This money is not taxable and is (in theory) enough to cover the basic needs of food, shelter and clothing. The idea is that once people are free from worrying how to "survive", they are more willing and able to become productive members of society.

I have been reading about Universal Basic Income (UBI) for many years now, and recently read an amazing book that does an in depth analysis of the idea, both from a philosophical viewpoint and a practical one. The book is entitled "Give People Money" by Anne Lowrey. In it, the author examines the finer points of where the idea is coming from, why it is a necessity and how we might implement its ideas.

The compelling argument brought forth in this book is the citing of numerous, real-world studies that actually implemented UBI programs in various parts of the world and what effect it had on the people who participated. The results were surprising and counterintuitive. Perhaps the author, in trying to make their point, gave a slightly rosy picture of the possibilities such a program could bring about, but, in general, most trials of this program had statistically positive results.

There are many who feel like this is a recipe for disaster as they insist that once people have no incentive to work, they will whither away and rot, or live lives that are self destructive and idle.

Jordan Peterson writes that money in the wrong hands is of little use, and that if you are a person who tends to be an idiot with money, giving you more of it just makes you a bigger idiot. He says,

> *"Even money itself may prove of little use. You won't know how to use it, particularly if you are unfamiliar with it. Money will make you liable to the dangerous temptations of drugs and alcohol, which are much more rewarding if you have been deprived of pleasure for a long period"*
>
> — 12 RULES FOR LIFE - JORDAN PETERSON

He even adds, you may be susceptible to con-artists and those higher on the dominance hierarchy who are likely to take advantage of you.

There is that word again. Dominance. Maybe the idea of UBI needs to be considered within the context of a partnership model. If we were to change our thinking as a society from one of competition and dominance to one of caring and cooperation, maybe the arguments against these programs would no longer hold water.

Riane Eisler argues against this policy as well. She believes that,

> *I believe that this opinion is just a description of how things are right now as a result of our behavioural programming up to this point. We have many smart people that can see the big picture. Implementing a UBI program should include a bit of education and/or social conditioning in addition to a fist full of cash.*
>
> — *THE REAL WEALTH OF NATIONS - RIANE EISLER*

Jordan Peterson has indicated that our need to do something important is built into our nature. We need a **purpose**. This is what makes us happy and gives us psychological peace. We need to strive for something bigger than ourselves. We need to belong to a collective of like-minded or similar people who share a common value or belief system. If we made it a point to teach our children the importance of finding purpose in life, then the arguments against UBI would start to lose their weight. People who are happy to live off of the spoils of other people's hard work have not really understood how to be happy. Changing an economic system is not just changing the math, it is changing ourselves too. We need to think differently as much as we need to act differently. Ms. Eisler suggests we need to start caring. Is caring not an idea? It is a way of thinking. This all begins with raising children properly with correct values, morals and psychological support. The information we need is already out there. We don't need to invent anything new at this point. We just need to implement the well-documented paradigms that are available today from exceptional thinkers.

Science has made tremendous sociological progress too, but this has been hard to propagate through the general populace because there are so many mental barriers to overcome in order to get people to learn new things. We have social norms, religious zeal, cultural bias and all sorts of "belief" systems that encumber our path to enlightenment. We need to accept that we are all humans and we differ very little at our core. We can adopt new ideas that benefit ourselves, our children and humanity in general if we are willing to accept input from the best and brightest.

I suppose my argument supports the old idea of:

"If you want to change the world, start by changing yourself"

So if we start developing a substrate of collective survival, where no-one goes without food, shelter and clothing, then building upon that with capitalist ambition, we could have the best of both worlds. Giving people money would allow them to participate at whatever level they are capable and willing to partake in. How people respond to this model has everything to do with what we teach them, who they have as role models, and what opportunities they have available, and less to do with what would happen today, using our outdated and dominance oriented belief systems.

GIVE THEM MONEY

Many people have argued against UBI stating that it would create a nation of entitled parasites, who contribute nothing to society and would be a burden on the system. At first glance, this seems pretty obvious, but the data derived from actual real world trials tells a different story.

https://tnc.news/2020/09/20/malcolm-universal-basic-income-fails-on-social-economic-and-moral-grounds/

Everyone is so concerned about who is going to pay for it. We cannot change a system and still think that the new one will continue using bad ideas from the old one.

We have the ability to invent a system that works for everybody. We just need to come up with ideas that make sense one their own, and not rely on the way it "used to work".

For instance, did you know that US banks were able to lend out 4 times more money than they actually had on deposit? This is what drives our modern economy, debt. There is not real currency anymore. Yet, we don't blink an eye at this. The banks are basically creating "money" out of thin air. They are lending "virtual" dollars in return for interest payments. These fake dollars are buying things in the real world. We invented this. We are all agreeing to believe that these fake dollars are worth something, so on it goes. Why can't we just invent the money to pay for UBI? It's sounds crazy, but we are already doing this in many ways.

The Iraq war was never actually paid for, according to Give them Money. The author claims that the war effort to fight Iraq in the 1990's was never budgeted for or paid back to anyone. It was all fake money. So why can't we use the same type of fake money to pay for UBI? We can conceive of ideas like debt forgiveness, fiat currency, overloading, and "market value". We should be able to collectively agree how to pay for UBI.

Universal health care is another example of a collective initiative that works. Canada and Great Britain have universal health care and everyone enjoys health care for free or very low premiums as part of their provincial health insurance. Because the health care providers are not "for profit" it works. It has it's issues, yes, but the last I checked, Canada and Great Britain were thriving capitalist societies with strong economies and healthy productive inhabitants. There is a marriage of formerly contrasting ideas to be had, we just need to stop finding road blocks that are leftovers from outdated paradigms.

We need to stop being so literal and start being creative..

- left brain vs right brain

- male vs female

..it's all the same. Let's use BOTH!

In most cases, giving money to people tends to help them. This, in turn, helps them help themselves. Most people who received a monthly stipend with no questions asked used the money for very practical and life-affirming things. They used it to take classes, or get child care so they could work more shifts. It enabled single mothers and caregivers more time to spend on themselves. Some even started small businesses.

I have heard about a few countries with social programs that incorporate individual components of this idea. For instance, in the city of Dohan , housing is free to its citizens. They enjoy an insane standard of living and one of the highest incomes per capita in the world. This is a capitalist country with an Islamic philosophical bias, yet they understand that taking care of its people is a priority. There are still people who rise above the free housing to own mansions etc. - there is no limit to the potential. They just don't have to start from zero.

UBI can take many forms, it doesn't have to always be money. It could be free basic housing, free groceries, free schooling, free healthcare, free basic clothing. It could be anything we decide helps lift people from poverty and give them dignity and enough freedom to realise their potential. The real world examples show this to be the case. As was suggested earlier, if UBI or some semblance of it can make people feel "safe" then they are far more likely to aspire to fulfil their potential instead of perhaps subduing their morality in order to do what it takes to survive.

These types of results are more typically "the rule" than "the exception". People in general want to be productive. They want to express themselves and contribute to the world. Idleness is not a universal goal. Ask any person, who has built a business and then sold it to lay under a palm tree and sip

Pina coladas, how long that lasted. They go crazy pretty darn quickly. Not because they are super high-achievers, but because we are wired that way as human beings. We desire, crave, and *need* **purpose**. Without purpose, we are miserable. A life with little to no strife quickly leads to rumination and depression. We need to be challenged.

A recent study found that suicide rates during the great depression were lower than they are now, in the era of prosperity never before seen on earth. The reason? Purpose. The people of the depression era had a singular purpose - to survive. Life was hard, and they had to find a way to make ends meet and feed themselves and their families. Because it was a struggle, they had no time for rumination. They were too busy trying to live through the day.

This may seem to make the opposite point of the theme of this book but hear me out. I am not saying that these people were happy to be struggling to survive. I am not in any way suggesting that maybe we need to forget prosperity because we will become fat, lazy and bored. I am saying that the human spirit is hard-wired to reach. We need to push our limits and realise our true potential. Giving people money would definitely enable a minority of folks to piss their life away, yes. They probably were going to anyways. But it may just be the catalyst to help the next Mozart or Einstein out of the streets and into the history books.

Therefore, in order to achieve our potential as human beings we would do well to have our basic needs taken care of. If we all received enough money to live on and didn't have to spend our time, effort and life energy on survival, we might be able to truly bring our gifts to the world. Who knows how many great works could have been created if a person only had the time.

Let's be honest, we all know the rule that,

"What one person gets for free, another person has to work for".

The idea is that the rich work hard and then get taxed to death to subside the lazy poor. This is not the way it actually works, in general, yet unfortunately there are a few people out there who do fit that mould. We all know people who don't work, exploit the system, and spend their days finding ways to scam their way through life. They spend more effort on finding ways to get out of paying for things than they do trying to earn a living. Yes, these people are out there but I might argue that some of them are that way because of the current state of the capitalist system, not a lack of morals.

There are also the people who are struggling with addiction. Giving these people money seems like a foolish thing to do as it would just accelerate their decent into oblivion. This might be the case, but we may want to consider the context this addiction behaviour is happing in. What if everyone knew they had a warm place to sleep for themselves and their family, no matter what. What if they knew that they would be fed and clothed and provided healthcare if they got sick, no matter what? What if this was a universal policy. Perhaps not having to worry about those things may take away some of the impetus to find an escape in the addictive behaviours. Worrying about money and having the responsibility to taking care of people can be a burden that is difficult to bear, especially if you are starting from behind.

The first thing to go out the window when you are struggling to survive is morality. You justify behaviours and decisions that you normally wouldn't, in the interest of finding a way to eat and pay the rent. Look around in most low income neighbourhoods and you will see crime, and addiction and subjective morals. It is the chicken and egg argument. Is the presence of questionable behaviours a result of poverty or is poverty a result of questionable morality? It is very hard to say. There are many factors, but I believe that you cannot discount a person's environment when it comes to what made them the way they are. If there is such a thing as systemic racism and systemic discrimination then this is not a small influence. It already is apparent that women have been discriminated against for a long time, and racism has been going on for a long time, and the fight to end these injustices had been moving along slowly. Yet, we cannot blindly say everyone has equal opportunity and everyone should just go to school and get good grades and attend a good college and get a good job and live the American dream. It is not readily available to everyone. That is the truth. Some people have a great many more obstacles to overcome in the pursuit of the American dream than others. We should not ignore this.

Giving people money is a way to try to allow people an equal starting point. Even social programs that provide food clothing and shelter to everyone would be a way to start. We need to think of people first, profit second. Capitalism can embrace BOTH competition and cooperation. We just have to think about it creatively and make it a part of our collective consciousness.

A caring economy, or as I like to put it "tempered capitalism", might allow for more human creativity and a higher standard of living for everyone.

It's worth thinking about.

One of the ideas here is that universal basic income is truly universal. Everyone gets it, regardless of income, and earning money through any other means does not reduce the amount that you receive. If you have a program that takes away from the stipend as you earn income it disincentivizes people to work. When you allow people to make as much money as they want and they will still receive enough to make ends meet, then it creates a whole different dynamic.

One of the interesting facts mentioned about UBI programs is that there is a statistically measurable improvement to overall mental health. The implications of this cannot be underestimated. When people are happier and less stressed, they are physically healthier, which reduces the burden on the health care system. When people are less stressed and happier they tend to commit less crime, take better care of themselves, and are less inclined to try to escape from their dire circumstances through drugs and alcohol.

No system is perfect and it would be unrealistic, if not unfair, to expect any system to fix *all* of societies ills.

None of this happens in a vacuum. We have to keep in mind that we are all connected in an infinite number of ways. Just like our bodies, if we fix one part, that benefit can be felt in other parts too, and vice versa. If we abuse our bodies physically, there is a mental toll to be paid. If we suffer mental illness, it often results in poor health as well. The world as a whole is no different.

Any changes we make to our society can be felt in other ways. New York City discovered that one of the most effective ways to reduce crime was to clean up the city. When people live in beautiful surroundings they tend to commit less crime. This is a proven fact. They planted trees and various plants, removed graffiti, fixed broken sidewalks and added community gardens to vacant lots. This created a sense of pride in the communities and the behaviour of the citizens changed.

I find it amazing that we can talk about urban planning in a book about money and personal finance. This just shows how things are always connected in ways we don't always expect. So the whole notion of UBI is hard to predict whether there will be negative or positive consequences until we do it. The studies have shown it to be mostly positive, and we can learn from those studies and try it out. We can refine it as we go along, fix the bugs and evolve it as we observe the results, positive or negative.

We already adhere to many socialist ideas without being too offended by them.

Hiways - We all pay taxes and that money goes towards building hi ways that everyone uses, in spite of how much each of us contributed to its construction costs.

The military - The military protects us all, no matter whether we paid in a lot or a little.

Welfare - There is some sort of government subsidy for those on the bottom of the economic ladder in most developed countries. Depending on where you live, it has different names.

Healthcare- Here in Canada and other countries, everyone gets free healthcare, no matter how much tax we paid.

I am sure there are many more examples. People are always so terrified to talk about social programs because it instantly reeks of "socialism" or "left wing" or some other "ism" that has failed miserably in the past. Yet we already are enjoying the spoils of social programs without questioning it, via the above mentioned services and others.

There are certain "careers" in the world that might be deemed "immoral " that exist solely because the need for money makes them seem justified:

Fishing for shark fins

Hunting elephants for ivory

Burning the rainforest to farm cattle

Human trafficking

I have to believe that the people engaging in these activities are driven by the need for money (survival) and didn't dream of being an "ivory poacher" when they grew up. Our current system of "every man for himself" creates these types of activities because people feel they don't have a choice. If everyone had the basics of life available to them they might also have new choices available as well . It seems like a luxury to be able to refuse to engage in morally questionable jobs. UBI may have the power to give people the option to choose.

I recently read a story in a book called "The Psychology of Money" about a man who made a fortune in the tech boom of the 1990s. He was so rich that one day he bought a stack of gold coins. He then proceeded to have a "coin skipping" contest with another man at the shore of the pacific ocean. He literally threw thousands upon thousands of dollars into the ocean just for fun. This story makes me slightly ill, as I can't believe someone would be that unbelievably wasteful and ignorant of the good that he could be doing with that wealth, instead of flushing it down the toilet.

But wait..

I am reminded of a story my wife told me. It was told to her by her yoga teacher who spent some time in India learning more about her craft. While she was there we was speaking to someone who asked her,

"Is it true that in your country everyone has fresh, clean water in your house?"

"Yes" she replied.

The person then asked incredulously,

"I hear you have so much fresh water that you actually pee in it. Is this true?"

She was embarrassed to answer but nodded in the affirmative.

Now I felt a little bit like the tech billionaire throwing gold coins in the ocean.

I was humbled by hearing this story because we take so many aspects of our life for granted. We are living in truly magical times, where we all enjoy luxuries like clean water and safe streets in most places, yet we don't realise that we are already rich. Perhaps we need to share the wealth. If everyone had access to these things world-wide then possibly their perspective could change too and they would have the opportunity to become all that they can be without spending their time and energy just trying to survive. Survival isn't even a question for those of us in the Western world, yet it is an everyday concern for many.

Instead of wishing we were living like billionaires, perhaps we could make sure everyone had the opportunity to eat and get an education. This is a socialist perspective, I am aware, and it rubs many the wrong way, but it is possible to shoehorn these kinds of ideas into our existing capitalist system. It doesn't have to be one way or the other. We can do both. We can lift up the individual while keeping the collective well-being in mind. There is a system that works. We just need to figure out what that looks like.

Another thing to keep in mind is the propensity for people to abuse the system. I see it all the time. People who take advantage of the welfare system, or the health care system because they figure out how they can get something for nothing. I believe this type of behaviour is fuelled by lack. People will abuse the system when they feel like it is necessary for their well-being. They equate money with life so they feel compelled to maximise their returns. I understand, but I am disgusted by those who think that the world owes them a free-ride. I am a very adamant believer in accountability. Everyone should contribute to society in some way. Either by paying taxes, or volunteering their time, we should all be required, expected and obligated to spend a portion of our capital output to the greater good. As is included in the Ubuntu Contributionism paradigm, everyone has a duty to give a little. If it is fair, we all give the same percentage of our resources, no matter what our station in life is in the moment. And if the calculations in the book are correct, and there is universal buy-in from everyone, no-one would be overburdened with their social obligations. 4 hours a week of un-paid service to social projects, or the equivalent in cash from each person would cover all of the needs of everyone. That sounds pretty doable to me.

I am not naive enough to believe there still won't be people who try to abuse the system, or take advantage of others, or commit crimes. People are still people, and we are not going to change human nature anytime soon, but if we can move towards the ideal, at least people can see the possibilities.

At the very least, we should teach these things in school. I have spent a great deal of time teaching people how to win at the game of money as it presently is constructed, yet I wonder why I need to do so. We have developed the "game" of money and forced everyone to play it, yet we neglect to teach everyone the rules. We need to put financial education as a requirement in the school syllabus as it is a requirement for life. More so than calculus. We need people to understand how money works, how it flows. We should have a class that not only teaches money management, but macro-economics, and perhaps different ideas about how we could approach the system.

I feel obligated to write this book because I realise that too many people are struggling financially, and it doesn't make sense that it is still so hard for so many people to have a comfortable existence in an age where we have the technology and resources to provide basic necessities to everyone without much effort. It is a poor system that places value on scarcity and neglects to value life.

By offering different ideas, I hope to at least make you think. I hope that we can spread the ideas and figure out how to change the world for the better by just propagating knowledge. No need for war or revolution. We just need to see what is possible, talk about how to implement the ideas and work together to bring them into reality. This is a peaceful and productive endeavour. Caring about people and our planet are not airy-fairy hippy ideals, they are necessities for our continued existence. We need to balance ambition with benevolence. We need to allow both mind-sets to coexist. I believe it is possible.

Chapter Six

MINIMALISM AND TINY HOUSES

I have become addicted to several YouTube channels that portray the lives of people who have decided to live "Alternative Lifestyles".

This covers:

1. Living off-grid
2. Living frugal lifestyles (minimalism)
3. Living in Tiny Houses
4. Living in camper vans (Van life)
5. Living in RVs
6. Building your own house

..and many more.

What I love about these "movements" as they are referred to, is that they all have a common theme of escaping the rat race or not buying into the American dream. I suspect these ideas arise out of the frustration and "quiet desperation" that our society of runaway inflation and unfettered capitalism creates. As I have mentioned before, everything costs money. The fact that you have to go to extreme measures to NOT have to spend money says something. As an example, in my city, there are no tiny houses, because they have made the laws so impossible that you cannot do it. You are not allowed to place your tiny home on vacant land as it changes the zoning and you must pay ridiculous taxes, and you cannot place it on someone else's land or they get dinged for rental taxes etc. They get you coming and going. They have designed it so that EVERYTHING is owned and must be paid for.

People who aspire to live frugally are sharing this info on social media because people are hungry for it. They want to live free. They want to only own what they need and not be consumers. This doesn't help the economy as it is currently structured so measures are in place to make this kind of living difficult. But people are figuring out that stuff doesn't make them happy. Experiences are far more valuable than things. Relationships are far more valuable. This is right in line with a caring economy in the sense that people are trying to figure out what they truly care about and make those things their priority, instead of buying things that advertisers tell them to.

An interesting tidbit that keeps popping up in the interviews with the full-time RV or "Van Life" people is that it is not necessarily an easy way to live, and that they still have problems. I suspect this is probably the way any lifestyle is, but the difference is these people say it is totally worth it. The sense of freedom, self-efficacy and sovereignty that they experience is worth any of the hardships they encounter. Imagine that. We live in a country that is considered "free", yet people are starving for the actual experience of freedom. We have become slaves to consumerism. We have become slaves to a lifestyle that has been thrust upon us by society, TV, movies, and our parents that we should own a nice car, a big house, live in the "Right neighbourhood" and send our kids to a "good" school. We are being told this everyday. Why do so many people feel like that life is akin to being in prison? Why do they not feel free?

The other common theme that these modern day nomads repeat is the best thing about their lifestyle is the people they meet along the way. The sense of community that they experience is one of their primary joys in life. These are not hermits or anti-social survivalists, these are normal happy people who are thrilled to be able to have a shared experience with other like-minded souls. It really hammers home the whole concept that "THINGS" were not making them happy, but experiences and other humans are the catalyst for a happy life. This "alternative" lifestyle is truly teaching these freedom-seekers to place value on things that are important. This is the start of something massive, I believe.

More and more people are waking up to the notion that our ideas about how life "should" be are not always the best way to go, and that there are other ways to be happy.

I love capitalism for its virtues and hate it for it's flaws. We need to re-think capitalism and perhaps make the changes necessary to bring people, relationships and life a higher status within its tenets. It is great for driving industry, innovations and productivity. We enjoy a higher standard of living than our ancestors did, due to its influence. By no means should we throw out the baby with the bathwater. Capitalism is necessary because it rewards hard work, creativity and merit. It is a wonderful incentive to get things done and keep score. However, we need to find a way to capitalise or value things that matter to the betterment of humanity not just to get rich. Being rich is a fine state of being, but it should not be the pinnacle of the value heirarchy. It is hard to be idealistic about this as money makes the world go around. As I have pointed out before, money equals life. We have to find a way to make money a means of exchange to quantify value, but allow it to flourish within the context of a humanitarian paradigm. We need to place capitalism as an equal partner with the social good.

Just as competition and cooperation should be seen as equally effective tools depending on the situation, and Men and Women and their underlying nature should be seen as equal partners in a healthy society, we need to devise a system whereby everyone has food, clothing and shelter at a minimum, while the ambitious are free to pursue any amount of wealth they desire. We need to find a way to temper the lust for wealth and power. As soon as wealth becomes exploitive or corrupt, it must be corrected. It tends to be in the nature of large organisations like corporations or governments to become corrupt. They slowly, over a period of time, tend towards corruption in small increments. Facism does not happen overnight, it sneaks up on you. Don't let it happen.

I think more and more people see this happening and want to do something about it. They are leaving the rat-race and are trying to simplify their lives. This is a great first step.

MINIMALISM

Stoicism is becoming more and more popular. People are finding peace and joy in having few possessions and not being chained to a desk or sitting under florescent lights all day. The old ways are fading. This is good.

As the world becomes more connected and more and more jobs are done via a computer, the "Laptop Lifestyle" is becoming a reality for many people. You can be a contributing member of society from just about any location where there is a stable internet connection. This simple technological change has opened the eyes of many people to a new way of living.

The COVID-19 pandemic accelerated this movement as the need to "work from Home" during quarantine became a necessity. Suddenly companies are realising that they can still be productive and have a useful workforce without the need for expensive office space. With the tools and software available today, there really are not many situations where you need someone to actually be sitting in a cubicle if their job is just done on a computer.

As runaway inflation has made the cost of housing, food, transportation, healthcare and education far too expensive for many people, these alternative lifestyles have had an interesting effect. Not only do these people learn to live on very little money and still have rich, full lives, they are making the need for the above expenses less important. Therefore, they may eventually go down in value in step with the old rules of supply and demand. If more people live frugally , traditional purchases such as houses and cars may become more attainable as the demand for them wanes.

Sadly, the price of RVs has gone up. Walmart is starting to not allow people in RV's to park in their parking lots overnight. This is the result of capitalism being more concerned with profit than people. But as people find ways to remove themselves from the "game" the system needs to change to accommodate the new normal. If the system is going to change anyways, let's steer it in the right direction. Let's understand our options and make it the way we want it. The independence and pioneering spirit of the minimalists and van-lifers is a testament to the will of people to not accept a broken system. This is yet another option in the fight to temper capitalism.

I seems to me that in a world where we are supposed to be "free" that we should be able to choose to play the game of money or not. Or at the very least, we should be able to choose to play at the scale that we feel suits our lives. If people want to live with very few possessions and spend their time in a 8X10 box then go for it. The system is designed for people to HAVE to participate, no matter how ill-prepared they are to succeed. I suppose it is because the government wants everyone to pay taxes to pay for infrastructure that they may or may not use, but I have suggested that this is a small part of a bigger problem The system is broken and the full time "van life" people have decided to change the rules.

Removing yourself from the world or refusing to acquiesce to the rules is one way to deal with the problems our current capitalist system has, but I think we are far better off trying to fix it. Capitalism is a wonderful philosophy that, in practice, has done far more good than harm. We should not put it on such a pedestal that we are afraid to see the chinks in the armour. Let's examine where it is potentially failing and see if we can come up with a better solution. The trap is, we start to think of Capitalism as some immutable God of nature that has a mind of its own and demands absolute obedience. We cannot forget that we (humans) thought up the idea of capitalism and that we can change it if it isn't serving us anymore. A world-wide religion, indeed.

So what can we do?

Chapter Seven

TEMPERED CAPITALISM

I have been preaching about how awesome capitalism is in my previous books and blog universe, but I always insert my personal caveat that capitalism is good if it has limits. It needs some checks and balances as a part of its use. It cannot run untethered or it will destroy us. It is a means for exchange. That is it. It is not our religion, yet it is the most adhered-to set of philosophical principles in the whole world. No matter your race, religion, creed or nationality, we all worship at the alter of money and capitalism.

Wars may appear to be the result of philosophical differences (to stop the spread of communism) or religious differences (the christian crusades) but if you dig a little deeper, it always comes down to money and/or power. There is little else that gets us riled up as much as money or the fear of losing it. People kill for money. People sacrifice their principals for money far too often.

Based on the ideas put forth by Ms. Eisler, I suspect it is not money in and of itself that is the cause. It is the paradigm of dominance or power that is the problem. Money represents life in many ways. Because we assume money and the system that beholds it is immutable and sacred, we allow the most horrible of atrocities to occur because we believe that it is some divinely decreed law that we are powerless to contradict.

MAKE IT THE WAY WE WANT IT

The fact is, we invented the whole thing .We all just agreed to this nonsense. All we have to do is agree to do it differently. It is simply a matter of deciding that we are going to value different things, and perhaps, put people, life, and the planet in a higher position in our values hierarchy than we have previously. It really is that simple. But why don't we? What is stopping us?

First of all - people don't like change. It is hard for people to move out of their comfort zones. They have a hard time learning new processes and procedures at work, let alone a whole new monetary system. People feel comfortable with what they know, it feels safe and familiar, even if it is fundamentally wrong. That is why many people stay in abusive or unhealthy relationships. It is less scary than the unknown.

Second of all - people don't know there are alternatives. If all you ever know is what you have seen and heard and experienced in your own life, and have not had exposure to other ideas, customs or beliefs, you will not necessarily even start to contemplate there is other ways to see the world.

It is no surprise that people who live in small towns in the middle of nowhere tend to be the least comfortable with "outsiders" - people who come from a different culture or have different skin colours. Why? Because it is unfamiliar. Simple as that. And people fear that which is unfamiliar, because they just don't understand it yet. It is not a conscious choice to be biased against things that are different or unfamiliar. It is actually built into our DNA. Studies have shown that people naturally are more comfortable with people who are like themselves. They trust them more, and they like them more. It is just the way it is.

Yet if you study people who live in cosmopolitan cities with a mix of people of different races, religions and customs, they don't even realise that prejudice is a thing. Even though, technically, these people are "different", there is a lot of "different" in their everyday world, so it is actually familiar.

WHO STANDS TO LOSE?

The biggest hurdle to changing our economic mindset is those who stand to lose in the new system. These people at the top of the old monopoly system will do just about anything to stay there. If you have been lucky, shrewd, blessed, or hard working enough to rise to the top, why would you ever willingly renege that which you have achieved? It seems unthinkable. Most rich people, contrary to popular belief, actually worked really hard to achieve their wealth and power and it would be morally suspect to force them to give it all up.

The problem here is that, nobody is asking them to give anything up. We are not suggesting we throw out the baby with the bathwater. Capitalism is a great differentiator against those with ambition and those without. A true meritocracy is not a bad thing, and I support it whole-heartedly. We need to allow those who are willing to work for it, and have the gumption to ethically accumulate it, to acquire a much wealth as they see fit to.

It just might be necessary to do it with a slightly different set of rules. The rules that we, collectively , as a species can come up with if we want to. Many economists today feel like the re-distribution of vast fortunes is really a necessity in order to keep the system running smoothly. When money pools in one place, it doesn't flow as it should, and the health of an economic system depends on the flow on wealth. As money is a means of exchange, it needs to be exchanged if it is to keep the economy going. People worth billions and billions of dollars are actually making the economy sick, if that wealth is just sitting there not being spent. I am sure there is an amount of money that is "Enough". We just need to figure out what that might be. How many gold-plated yachts does a guy need?

The opposition to a caring economy is not necessarily the people with money, it just might be the people with power. The powerful of this world stand to lose if there are less wage slaves to do their bidding.

I love how in the "Lord of the Rings" series the whole quest was centered around a ring. The ring of POWER. Not the ring of wealth or the ring of "really really good looking". As stated in the book "for men crave power above all else". This was a very insightful statement by JRR Tolkien. It is true. Power is the one thing that people hate to lose, and are reluctant to give. No-one wants to bend a knee to anyone else unless there is a good reason or they have no choice. We seem to be more than happy to give people money for things we don't need to impress people we don't like. But we rarely give up power. And because money is a world-wide religion, and represents our very survival, having money tends to come with a certain amount of power.

Some would say that power is taken, not given. I am not so sure. No-one can have power over you unless you agree to it. They may threaten you with all kinds of terrible things, but you still have the choice as to whether you succumb.

I believe that the world has been designed like a monopoly game for so long, that the "winners" at the top are quite determined to keep it that way and not allow the masses to rise above their station or the people at the top will loose their "elite"status. They are fed a steady stream of money from those who don't understand the system and they will do anything to keep the status quo because it benefits them.

When we label the two sides as Domination vs. Cooperation, we can imply many things from the word domination. Domination denotes power over others. It unfortunately has been associated with men and male privilege for a long time, and I am sad to say the judgement is well deserved. People like Ruth Bader Ginsberg had to fight for women to be treated equally because male dominance had run amok.

The problem here is that we have spilled over the male dominance paradigm into all facets of life. Especially money. Wealth and capitalism tend toward competition and it is seen as weak, airy-fairy, or communist to suggest that it could be otherwise. Yet I believe it can be. I believe just as our minds are changing about how men and women can coexist as equal, yet different, members of the human race, capitalism and certain socialist ideas can exist in harmony as well. Some countries already live this way. Sweden is a good example.

At a basic level, the people who have learned and become adept at the "game" of money are reaping the benefits of their wealth creation skill-set and would have no reason to change the game. I can appreciate this. I have written several books that give concrete step by step instructions to win the game as it exists right now. But not everyone has the aptitude or the opportunity to excel at the game. Should these people who have not read my books, had rich parents, found a mentor, or had enough stability in their life to survive be punished for their circumstances? Should they be left to "die" just because they couldn't play the game very well for whatever reason? It seems a little harsh to accept that you must play the game of money well or you will perish. That is the mindset we find ourselves in. It is based on competition as a foundational belief. It is saying "we learned the rules of the game and executed our game plan well so we win and the rest of you losers can suck it." This is not a sustainable approach to anything. As Monopoly taught us, this will eventually leave all but a few destitute in more ways than one.

Ultimately, we are battling against ourselves.

We create these ideologies and sociological structures and we then make them into immutable gods- we attach so much "meaning " to these ideas that we refuse to change them for fear of collapsing the very foundations of our existence.

We seem to require a "scaffolding" of belief to build our chaotic everyday reality around even though we were the ones who made up the idea to begin with.

Tim Ferriss, in his book "Tools of Titans" includes a conversation with an army general, Jocko Willink. He is talking about having a structured life where by we are happiest when we have some sort of commitment everyday. Tim Ferriss, who lives the lifestyle of the "new Rich" took the concept in a slightly different direction but made a great point. He applied this concept to the lifestyles of the financially independent. If you worked hard, and finally made it, you have a newfound "freedom". The most compelling (and insidious) freedom you have gained is time freedom - you can now do anything you want with your day. This state of being drives many people mad. They are unhappy and suffer existential angst due to the lack of structure in their lives. They worked for this, now they can't enjoy it. It is just because they need the structure or a foundation of commitment..

> *"I interpret this to mean, among other things, that you can use positive constraints to increase perceived free will and results. Freeform days might seem idyllic, but they are paralysing due to continual paradox of choice (e.g., "What should I do now?") and decision fatigue (e.g., "What should I have for breakfast?"). In*

> *contrast, something as simple as pre-scheduled workouts acts as scaffolding around which you can more effectively plan and execute your day. This gives you a greater sense of agency and feeling of freedom."*
>
> — TOOLS OF TITANS - TIMOTHY FERRISS

When people make a commitment to something, preferably with an attached meaning of "greater than themselves" they become more happy. Contributing to charity or trying to make significant changes in the world become a source of joy. Not because of the cause, but because it gives them a sense of safety. We need that foundation of meaning. We need that scaffolding, as Mr. Ferriss calls it. We require a context in which to exist. Some would call it a "PURPOSE".

I first saw this piece of wisdom on a cup of coffee in Starbucks:

> *"The irony of commitment is that it's deeply liberating -- in work, in play, in love. The act frees you from the tyranny of your internal critic, from the fear that likes to dress itself up and parade around like rational hesitation. To commit is to remove your head as the barrier to your life."*
>
> — — ANNE MORRIS

I THINK it applies to what we are talking about here.

We need the rules to live by, but we are the ones who made the rules.We are genetically programmed to worship or place ourselves at the mercy of imaginary constructs that we place higher ideals upon. Or so it would seem.

Religions, laws, traditions and even etiquette are all examples of ideas that some people live and die by but are man-made ideas that we came up with, they are not immutable laws of nature.

We are fighting against our own propensity to follow rules without questioning their efficacy or who invented them in the first place, and to what end. Always ask, "Who stands to benefit from this rule"? If it is a small subset of humanity who enjoy the benefits of the rule while ignoring or even feeding upon the remainder of our species, then the rule should be questioned - at a minimum. This is how oppression and discrimination are allowed to continue, because they clothe themselves in the uniform of "rules" or "the law" and we immediately hesitate to oppose or even question them.

So let's create rules that work for everyone and then follow them

The cure for many mental health issues is to create a new set of rules to live by

Alcoholics need to follow strict abstinence rules in order to get well - if you give them a choice they will make the wrong decision- we all cannot be left in a free form world where there are no rules, it would be anarchy- we only seem to function effectively if we have a set of rules to guide us whether implied or explicit. So why reinvent the wheel? We are not very likely to change our nature, so it makes sense that we can set ourselves up for success by creating new rules or paradigms that support us and help us all flourish. Just create new rules that benefit everyone and it is likely that we will mostly follow them, as we tend to put more stock in the stories we tell ourselves about reality than objective reality itself. We need rules, but we also need to know when to break them, change them or discard them altogether. We have a moral imperative to do so.

There is a better way to structure capitalism and our free society. We just need to get out of our own way.

Chapter Eight

POWER VS. WEALTH

Can we stop competition? Why would we want to? That would be counterproductive. Adopting anti-competitive behaviours would just be the pendulum swinging too far the other way. The partnership model or the cooperation model does not pit one against the other or make one philosophy the master of the other. The partnership model makes both philosophies equal partners. There are situations where partnership or cooperation are the most effective methodologies. There are others where domination or competition will work much better. The key is to have mutual understanding and respect for each mindset. The benefit of all people is a product of both working in tandem. The outcome of a pure competitive model is one winner and many losers. The outcome of pure cooperation is aimlessness and chaos.

PROCESS OR OUTCOMES

I am aware if you start to dissect the cooperation vs competition debate you can find yourself tumbling down some deep, dark rabbit holes. Not everything in this world can be delineated cleanly. We are human, after all, and we tend to generalize and fill in the blanks whenever possible.

I will put forth that cooperation and competition are not only *methods* to interact in the world but also possible *outcomes*. We can use one or the other methods to attempt to achieve an end. We can also define the endgame within each context.

Team sports are a good analogy. Players on a team compete against another team by cooperating with their own teammates (most of the time). The end goal is to win. So I would define this outcome as a competitive outcome, or there is one winner and one loser. This outcome is good for one team, bad for the other.

As I mentioned before, the game of Hanabi seeks to have everyone win the game. The outcome is cooperative, in a sense that everyone wins (or everyone loses).

If you were to change the objective of a game from winning to some other outcome, like "everyone having fun" or "everyone getting to touch the ball", then it would be a cooperative outcome. You can compete or cooperate to achieve this outcome, just as you can use either mode to achieve a win.

I bring up this point to clarify that the economic model being presented here is one of a cooperative outcome intertwined with a competitive outcome. How we get there will probably require a great many types of behaviours, including competition when necessary. We cannot dampen the human spirit. We want to encourage those who are driven to do great things to to them. Those who are unable or unwilling to do great things will still be a part of society, but will not be forced to play a game they may not be equipped to play.

Research proves that at least 25% of the people will

perform terribly in a competitive environment. This is not an insignificant number. There is a vast body of work that has explored these two forces and almost all have concluded that neither approach works well in every situation. We must value and be adept at both modalities.

Jordan Peterson sites studies in his book that claim human beings (like lobsters) naturally arrange themselves into hierarchies. It is suggested that this is wired into our DNA. I have also heard it claimed (by not so legitimate sources) that we may be wired genetically to naturally succumb to authority figures. We may even be prone to worship those we perceive as "above us" in some way (intellectually, spiritually, financially, or sadly even "better looking").

If this is the case, then we need to think critically about these studies or perhaps revive the nature vs. nurture debate. Maybe we are "hard-wired" to form hierarchies because we have just lived under the patriarchal/dominator rules for so long. This would not surprise me, if the responses I hear when I talk about this stuff are any indication. ("But then, who wins?") Perhaps it is not genetic, but learned behaviour. I always come back to the analogy that a fish doesn't know it is in water. If you live in a society that universally accepts certain beliefs as "true", why would you ever question them? You may not even realise there is an alternative. When people look at me like I am speaking a foreign language when I first start to talk about this stuff and they eventually begin to nod their head in understanding, I see that this is something that they just didn't think about before. There is no way I could know that they just naturally believe that the only approach to anything is to compete *or* cooperate.

"What does it take to succeed? This question has fuelled a long-running debate. Some have argued that humans are fundamentally competitive, and that pursuing self-interest is the best way to get ahead. Others claim that humans are born to cooperate and that we are most successful when we collaborate with others.

In FRIEND AND FOE, researchers Galinsky and Schweitzer explain why this debate misses the mark. Rather than being hardwired to compete or cooperate, we have evolved to do both. In every relationship, from co-workers to friends to spouses to siblings we are both friends *and* foes. It is only by learning how to strike the right balance between these two forces that we can improve our long-term relationships *and* get more of what we want.

So the question on my mind is really not how can we change the world, but how can we change the world without destroying it first. I ask this as per the title of this book because it is a possibility not only physically but conceptually. We might have to destroy the whole system of economics in order to rebuild it, just like some people believe we won't save the planet until we destroy ourselves first.

So the plan is to give each mindset it's due. There are certain situations where competition is necessary and certain ones where cooperation would be more effective - not unlike war and diplomacy. True diplomacy is not asking for what you want with the implied threat that we will blow you to bits if you don't acquiesce. It is truly wanting an outcome that is beneficial to both parties. A real, honest to goodness win/win. Otherwise it is intimidation and we are back to our old domination model. When it works for you, you tend to go back to the old reliable methods.

That is often why some politicians run on a platform of "traditional" values , which is actually code for "Male dominated society". This is what makes people feel safe, because it is familiar, instead of the hippy-dippy new ideas touted by left-wing intellectuals that use big words and read the New

Yorker. It doesn't always have to be that polarised. The true way is adaptation. The real solution is being smart and flexible enough to know which tool to use in the right situation. Sometimes we can go forward with an eye on getting everyone what they want. We can have time to think and understand our adversary in order to come to a mutually beneficial end. Sometimes we need to react swiftly and perhaps even violently to keep ourselves alive and prevent more harm from coming to others. We regret that situation but it is unfortunately necessary sometimes. The point is we need to have more than one tool in the toolkit. We need to approach life and economics and everything else with an adaptable frame of mind. If we are to move forward and evolve and find a harmonious coexistence with people, nature and the cosmos, we sometimes need to try to find a partnership, instead of trying to win. Not all situations are winnable or are even a game of that particular nature.

MONEY WORSHIP

I have often wondered at the way people view money as a measure of "how well you are doing" - we greet people with that question all of the time

"How are you doing?"

Is this a question about health, wealth, or happiness? A little of each I suspect, but the key here is how much we equate money with life itself.

Money is the only true religion that EVERYONE agrees upon. And I call it a religion because people take it as seriously as religion, maybe even more so. When people say things like "Its not personal, its business" and "I'm sorry we have to lay you off (so we can make our numbers and I get my bonus) it starts to make sense how much to we value money.

Let's look at a few examples.

In the western world, our society is designed so that you need money to survive. LITERALLY. If you have no money you will die. Yes there are some pathetic social programs like welfare and unemployment insurance that might help you survive, but the fact is these programs give you money to survive. You still have to pay money for food and shelter and clothing etc. No one gets it for free, NO ONE> I can hear you saying in your head right now,

"OF course not. Why would anyone get anything for free? I don't get anything for free, why should they?"

You see? We all believe nothing is, or should be, free.

Why not?

Isn't there enough to go around?

Another example is health care. Health care costs money. Doctors and nurses and health care professionals all take care of you for money. No-one does it for free. So if no-one got paid to take care of you when you needed it, you would die. These people will not do it for free. In places where there is universal health care, people don't have to pay for health care (they do, just in the form of high taxes), but the health care system is still doing what they do for money. It just comes from the government (Taxes), not the customers bank accounts directly.

So we all agreed that:

Money talks and bull*** walks.

WE NEED MONEY TO SURVIVE.

Absolutely everything has a price.

These are just some of the strange ideas about money we have all agreed to believe.

So the real questions that arise from this are;

1. What determines something's value?
2. What are people willing to pay?
3. Who stands to benefit from this system?

I know question 3 is a little out there, but I'm getting to it.

What determines something's value? In a true free market, as espoused by Martin Friedman, the market itself determines value based on supply and demand. It is an unemotional, fact based, non biased system of pure math. It's business, not personal.

So perception of value is the determining factor, theoretically.

So if I asked you what is the most valuable thing you have? You may say your home, or your family or your Mercedes, until I put a gun to your head. Then your answer changes. It becomes strikingly apparent that most valuable thing you have is your life.

So if your life is the most valuable thing you have, then allow me to suggest that that feeling is fairly universal. I would suggest that almost everybody on the planet values their own life quite highly. So, if this is the case, and we as a human race share that value, then shouldn't we also value other lives? Or even an abstract concept that human life is what makes the world go around, not money?

Riane Eisler makes the argument that we need to start placing value on life itself, therefore caregiving, child rearing and the planet itself all need to be given a much higher value as these are the things/people that make life happen. What could be more valuable than:

-Making people

-Taking care of people so they don't die

-Teaching people to be good people

-Teaching people to be productive members of society

-Not destroying the earth so that we all can keep producing.

Our current economic system is based on valuing dumb

things like GDP and economic growth. Quarterly profits and pure business stuff.

The people in power have slowly indoctrinated us to worship money over the truly valuable things so that we become slaves to a system that they control. When you control all of the money and have unlimited amounts of it you can control the population because we believe in the power of money so much we don't dare question it. We have more than enough resources and ingenuity to feed, clothe and house everyone on the planet without breaking a sweat. Yet we refuse to do it because we believe in the power of the economic system of haves and have-nots so much that we can't conceive of such a crazy idea as taking care of each other. That is too foreign a concept to be taken seriously.

Maybe we need to think about this for a minute. We could decide, collectively, to make it an imperative that:

- Everyone is fed
- Everyone is sheltered
- Everyone is clothed
- Everyone is educated
- Everyone has equal opportunity to make the most of themselves.

That is not an impossible task. In fact, it would take very little of the world's GDP TO MAKE THAT A REALTY. Yet we don't do it because that is "soft" or "Communism" or unsustainable. I'm here to tell you that our current system is unsustainable. We will run out of resources if we don't stop relying in growth as our major economic health indicator.

Ms. Eisler refers to this new way of thinking as a "caring economy". She is on to something. But I think there may be something more sinister at play here.

I believe we need to change the economic system to be more caring or more cooperative so that we can see our own brainwashing. We need to wake up to our blind adherence to the "way it is" and start to think that we, collectively as a human race, can choose something better. We can create an economic system that benefits everyone, just like Ms. Magie's board game. We fight this idea because we have been living in a domination/competition world for so long. We have been trying to worship money. We know for a fact that people are exploited and killed for money all the time. Some people out there feel that it is OK to value wealth over a human life. This is so absolutely wrong I don't even have the words to express it. Yet, there are many who do believe it. Without question.

SO WHO STANDS TO BENEFIT?

Let's pretend that there is this new designer drug called "money" Let's get everyone hooked on it. Now we control the supply of the drug, the laws surrounding the drug and we have unlimited supplies of it. People will do just about anything to get a hold if this drug. They can't function in the world without it. We now have a slave population to do our bidding, Those at the top of the power structures have known this for a long time. That is why slowly, over time, things have become more and more "Capitalistic" and less and less "Community" oriented. Inflation is making us more and more dependant on money and less able to be free.

INFLATION IS OUT OF CONTROL

We get less value for each dollar earned and more expenses. We have made surviving harder and harder to do. So if eventually everyone has to dedicate their every waking minute to surviving by somehow earning money, we have truly become a race of slaves to those elite few who have control of the money. And we do it willingly, because we agreed to hold money in such high esteem. We have collectively given money a life of its own, and forgot that it was just supposed to be a means of exchange. It was a representation of the human capital that we brought to the world. We value less and less the things that matter and become more and more seduced by the economic machine. Numbers and math and GDP and earnings per share all become our gods and we agree to bend a knee to their unfettered power..

Simon Sinek makes a good example in his book - a company saying that they can justify any action, even if it is inconsistent with their mission statement, is ok because it is not breaking any laws. Mr. Sinek punctuates this idea by comparing it to someone saying that it is ok to cheat on your spouse because it is not against the law - allowing someone to suffer or die because they don't have money is the same thing - a caring economy is a necessary change - we seem like we are mighty and powerful as a species but we will drive ourselves into extinction because we refuse to adapt - the rich and powerful won't renege power and wealth. I get it, but we need to make different things valuable if we are to survive - even overpopulation could be solved if we took care of each other. Most first world nations have a negative birthrate because they are educated, have healthcare, are relatively safe and respect women. In fact, some predictions show the world's population will naturally start to decrease as we become more prosperous.

Two generations of people having two or less children, which is the norm in G7 nations, would make a huge impact on the population in a positive way and allow a higher standard of living for everyone. Prosperity tends to bring with it better health, less war and conflict, less domestic violence, and education. Education alone brings critical thinking and less superstition, so a decrease in outdated cultural practices that demean women, forbid birth control, and place men on a pedestal just because they are male, could be re-thought.

We need to stop acting on the letter of the law and start getting the spirit of the law. We probably should even change the laws to better serve humanity as a whole because we made up the laws in the first place.

Humanity is what it is all about, not money.

Chapter Nine

YOU BECOME WHAT YOU THINK ABOUT

"When I was doing "Outliers" I was struck by how often when successful people described their lives, they would talk about the things that went wrong or the things that were hard, as opposed to the things that were easy or went right. "

-Malcom Gladwell

I am fascinated by how certain ideas are presented by different authors or teachers at different times and in different contexts, yet share a universal theme. I consider this theme more likely to be a fundamental truth. When I see something said over and over again by smart people from different walks of life, I tend to pay attention.

One of these ideas is that of "Long term perspective" . It has been suggested as one of the most powerful ways to truly make an impact on the world, yet it seems that our world does everything it can to not support that mindset anymore.

There is a study from Harvard, cited in the book "The Unheavenly City", by Edward C. Banfield, where a study was performed over many years to see what factors would be correlated to a person's success. They studied a graduating class of Harvard MBA students and tracked them over the course of their lifetimes. They periodically questioned them about many factors that were a part of their lives and tried to determine what particular traits or privileges would most contribute to their success over time. Of course, I've already given you the answer, long term perspective. But would you have guessed that? Not me. I would have guessed:

1. Family money
2. Good looks (yes this is an advantage)
3. Intelligence
4. Connections
5. Work ethic
6. Race
7. Gender
8. Choice of spouse
9. Charisma

Apparently the study found no real correlation between the above list and success. The most successful people were all over the map when it came to the obvious factors, but the only consistent trait that guaranteed success was long term perspective.

Long term perspective is the ability to see the big picture and make decisions based on how this will affect things over a long period of time and not pursuing quick fixes or instant gratification. I have written about this before, but now I have a larger perspective on it. I see how it is such a fundamental, powerful and universal idea that it applies to life in general not just financial success.

People today tend to skirt long term thinking because we really don't have to use it very often. Our lives have become so easy and instant that we tend to believe that everything should be easy and instant. We are bombarded with stories of 20 year old internet billionaires and overpaid athletes, rappers and movie stars that all seem rich and successful without a ton of effort (apparently). We glamourise the "exceptions" and forget about the rule.

The rule is, most millionaires took twenty years or more to become rich. They worked at it over a really long time, in a business that they usually started from scratch. They persevered and sacrificed and earned it. This is unheard of in our world, where you can have just about anything with the press of a button. True value is still hard to create, but we rarely hear about it or have the opportunity to truly appreciate it.

Simon Sinek in his book "The infinite Game" talks about long term perspective but he calls it an "infinite" mindset vs. a "finite" mindset. As he describes it, it is the ability to make business decisions on larger, more universal ideals than quarterly profits or short term gains. It is sticking to a true corporate value proposition and trying to build something that lasts and provides value that the world actually needs. It is treating employees as human beings instead of "head count". It is believing in a bigger goal than shareholder satisfaction.

Riane Eisler talks about the caring economy, and that philosophy is quite obviously in line with long term perspective. If we valued what truly mattered, instead of just the bottom line, we would start applying value to caregiving, human growth, human potential and the environment. Making economic decisions that place a high priority on these things and the human condition in general, instead of the dog eat dog , winner take all mentality, would be a very good example of

a. Long term thinking
b. Infinite Mindset
c. A "Caring economy"
d. A balance between competition and cooperation

As is often the case, the macro world and the micro world are reflections of each other. If we, as a society and as a species, are obligated to start thinking bigger, then the same ideals may be beneficial to us as individuals too.

What if we started to think bigger? What if we started to make decisions for the long term instead of trying to find a quick fix for everything or instant results? What if we started to plan our strategies over our lifetimes, or even generations?

I suggested in my first book "BYOB - Be Your Own Bank" that this is exactly what the rich elite do. They plan their whole financial world around generational wealth creation. They are thinking about their heirs and keeping the family money intact. When you start to think about investing over centuries instead of months or years or even decades, your strategy changes a little bit.

When you try to build a dynasty, you spend time thinking about a lot of things that make sense only in the context of generations. Are you going to invest in that hot new tech startup, or are you going to invest in a bank that has paid dividends consistently for over a hundred years?

If you are taking care of your life from a long term perspective, you make decisions differently. You don't do a crazy fad diet every few months, you eat right, exercise and do it consistently over a long period of time. You realise that good habits, performed over a long period of time create sure results that last. You realise that investing consistently over your whole working life and teaching your children how to invest is how your family lifts itself out of poverty and finds financial freedom for yourself and future generations.

I won't go into this too much as I have written about it before, but the ideas that are going to change the world and your personal world are universal. They are about seeing the big picture. They are about lifting your head up from your limited view of the game and seeing it from a different perspective. We all can learn something new. I love to learn and I read constantly. Every time I learn something new that

I can apply to my life I am thrilled to death about it. I feel like when I know something that I didn't know before I am now a new person. I feel like I am now more than I was. I feel like I am more effective and am more capable of making a difference in the world .

My quest as an author in all of my books, courses, website and blog is to inspire people to grow. I have enjoyed the process myself so much that I want to share it with others. I know how it feels to learn something new and feel like I have a plan that maybe I was struggling with before. I love to be taught the inside workings of previously mysterious things. I love to learn how things work and get new ideas from people smarter than me. I appreciate the hard work and deep thinking that went into many of the books I have read. I am more than happy to build upon someone else's twenty or thirty years of trial and error and use their strategies and insights to further my own ambitions.

So as Malcom Gladwell says, successful people tend to remember the struggles more than the successes. Why? Because they learned from them. They grew. They become more. More capable, more wise. They learned why many rich people say that they don't care if they lose it all because they know how to make it all back. That is true wealth. The knowledge of "how" to do it.

Don't get me wrong, I have been talking about a whole new way of looking at the world of money, but I still believe it is important to first learn how to play the game as it is presently. None of these ideas I am taking about are going to happen overnight. I believe that we need to learn how to make money and set ourselves up for success in the context of present-day reality.

If we have given ourselves the gift of financial freedom, we are now in a position to start to change the world. We cannot be very effective proponents of change and reform if we are struggling to survive. It is really hard. It takes a lot of energy, both mental and physical, to keep a roof over your head when you are financially struggling. It is a vicious cycle that is difficult to get out of. Only by educating ourselves and changing our mindset to a long term perspective can we get out of the cycle.

It is the old saying

> "The problems that exist in the world today cannot be solved by the level of thinking that created them.."
>
> — ALBERT EINSTEIN

This is the same thing. If you are struggling financially it might be that you are making short term decisions because you don't know any other option. If you take the time and invest in yourself, and start to plan for the long term, you can achieve amazing things, but it won't happen overnight, and it won't be easy. And it will be nearly impossible if you don't have the knowledge to do it. It all starts with learning. Either from books, courses, or people who have done it already, you can leverage their knowledge and experience to make the same things happen in your life.

We are more powerful than we realise. Sometimes it takes courage to change and find the strength or discipline to take a stand. Everyone's circumstances are different and I appreciate that sometimes people's challenges seem pretty darn insurmountable. But if you don't know another way to act, then you have no options. At least give yourself an advantage by learning about money and personal finance and investing and how the world works. Then you have the tools. Then it is up to you to use them or not.

CLASS STRUGGLES

One of the things that being wealthy brings is the practice of paying other people to do stuff you don't want to do. It is a perk of being rich to have people, who are lower in standing than you, to wait upon you. We see the world of the upper class in shows like Downton Abby where the wealthy lords are waited upon by an army of servants who work for minimal wages and spend their lives toiling while the elite attend dinner parties and dress for afternoon tea. It is an interesting dilemma to those who come from humble beginnings to have people wait on them as they were once the ones doing the serving. They feel uncomfortable in that situation whereas people who always had money think nothing of it. The question I have is, "is this morally appropriate"? Is it morally correct to have a society where the rich are waited upon by the poor? Well, in a sense, it might be the wrong question. The right question would be, are the people waiting upon the wealthy there by choice? That is the fundamental question. If they were there because they had no other choice, then the situation is flirting with indentured servitude which basically amounts to slavery. This should never happen and I could never support a system that perpetuates that. However, if someone's vocation is a choice, based on interest, aptitude or ambition (or lack thereof) then is is perfectly acceptable and I am all for it. The problem then becomes, whether the elite or the "help" are aware of the "Choice" and are willing to accept either lifestyle as an option, based on merit. The problem is when people with money feel they are "better" than those without it, or as is common in todays political arena, the unconscious benefits of "white privilege".

If we all have a common starting point, there is no such thing as classes, just merit.

PSYCHOLOGY VS. SOCIOLOGY

There is always the age-old struggle between a psychological view of the world and a sociological view of the world. The power of the individual vs. The power of social structures.

As I have suggested with the help of the smart people I have referenced, there is a model that integrates both points of view. Both paradigms have their place and both are useful when used in the right context. It is men respecting women and women respecting men. Neither has the upper hand. Each situation that presents itself requires either the hand of justice, the hand of mercy or a combination of each. We can learn to welcome, appreciate and respect the opposing nature of the two philosophies and call upon one or the other when we need them.

The first step is learning to accept the other point of view as valid and necessary. Like I stated earlier, a hammer thinks everything is a nail. A person who is competitive by nature thinks everything needs to be competed for. They must win.

A cooperative person believes all situations can be handled calmly and everyone can get along. This is not always the case, and they have a hard time digging in to a fight when necessary. It is also hard to know which approach is going to work and when to switch gears.

That is part of life and being human. I believe that will always be our struggle, but the first and most important step is to actually know that there are more ways to deal with the world than our default. In business, social interactions and government, we can always adhere to the balanced approach and see how each mode of being has its place and should be celebrated for its unique gifts and abilities in each situation.

Chapter Ten

THE ENDGAME

WHAT DO WE WANT?

When we look at "isms" that have failed throughout history it becomes interesting to note that a large part of the reason for their eventual demise was the underlying adherence to a domination model that they were built upon.

Communism - was an appealing idea to some, but not everyone is airy fairy enough to buy into it. Someone eventually wants to dominate and assume control. When a system that is designed for the collective good gets taken over by someone who wants to "win" it is doomed to failure.

Socialism - This tends to be just another fancy word for communism. When we offer lip service about the "people" but still retain a power elite in control of everything, we are still doomed. Power is not ever going to be given up freely or willingly. There is too much at stake to the people on the top.

Ubuntu - The hippies had the right idea, but once again, without clear hierarchy , nothing gets done and there is chaos. Studies have shown there needs to be hierarchy in order for society to function.

Democracy - Who doesn't love democracy? It's great. But what does it have to do with economics? Governing and politics are not synonymous with economics, even though most people think they are one and the same.

Capitalism - Now we are talking. The capitalist system is an idea that works quite well. It allows for a free market that fluctuates based on supply and demand. However, it is a cold-hearted system that does not really account for the human element.

As a species, our job here is to survive. Then once we have achieved that, we wish to thrive. Once we do that, we are free to ruminate ourselves into all kinds of intellectual and philosophical black holes. But one thing is clear; we need each other. We had learned that it is much easier to survive, thrive and ruminate if we do it together. Many hands make light work.

I would suggest to you that we have collectively reached a point in our existence on this planet where we have the knowledge and resources to ensure that every single person could feel safe. Every person could be feed, clothed and sheltered if we chose to make that a priority. It is an existential imperative. It would require a change in thinking from "I need to take care of me" to "We need to take care of each other AND take care of me".

I know it sounds like pie in the sky right now, but it is certainly possible. It just requires us to think differently - there is no other obstacle. It is not a matter of money. There is plenty of money for things that we deem important. It is not about logistics. There are plenty of systems in place to facilitate money distribution.

It is about the idea that we need to place importance on the right things. It is waking up from the nightmare of a world where it is "dog eat dog" and "every man for himself", a world where competition is the only way business works, to a world where competition and cooperation work side by side to advance the human race beyond our current circumstances.

We just need to spread the information. That is why I am writing this book. I really am trying to just insert an idea into people's heads that we can change the world just by thinking about it differently. If enough people start to value things that benefit us all, like the environment, or the well-being of people from other countries/cultures, we could all walk together through the doorway of enlightenment and gaze upon a new world where we are free to reach our highest potential, without the burden of survival on our collective backs.

Strangely, these ideas are not new, nor are they particularly abstract. People much smarter than me have written about these things for decades. Pioneers have developed social experiments to explore these concepts many times. Yet, every time I speak to someone new about these ideas they struggle to initially conceive of a world where competition isn't the primary paradigm of behaviour.

I suggested a concept of tempered capitalism in previous books, but I think it needs to be expanded. Instead of tempering capitalism, lets consider for a moment a possible "hybrid" economic system where we take the best of each idea and fit them together in a way that possibly strives towards the highest good of everyone. - not just the people at the top, who are the best at the game.

If we start by building a foundation of safety, where we put in place social policies where everyone is fed, clothed and housed, without cost. This would remove the uncertainty that creates selfish and/or desperate mindsets.

Once everyone is taken care of, we place a cap on inflation pertaining to basic necessities of life.

Then we gently place good old fashioned capitalism on top of that foundation. Once people are no longer working to survive, they will work for something far more inspiring. You are free to achieve, earn and accumulate as much wealth as you please. I cannot, in good conscious, let go of the idea of a meritocracy, whereby good hard working people are rewarded for their individual efforts to get ahead.

It has been suggested that overpopulation is a result of poverty. People tend to have lots of babies because they are playing the odds that eventually maybe one child will be successful and they can help out the family. Or maybe that creates more income for the family. I don't know. Some, like Riane Eisler suggest that in some cultures and impoverished nations there is a lack of education or access to birth control. She also suggests that women are still considered a lower class of human being and do not have the right to make choices for themselves as they are considered the property of their husbands. Ms. Eisler makes it very clear that empowering women is good for the economy in just about every instance.

If this is the case, then perhaps we can make a difference there too. By spreading new ideas through books and the internet about new ways of thinking and living, future generations can adopt these ideas as self-evident and shed the old customs that keep one half of our population in subjugation. I've seen it happen here with racism and homophobia, I am convinced it can happen anywhere - about anything. Nothing is as powerful as an idea who's time has come.

The pen just may be mightier that the sword.

SOME COLLECTIVE IDEAS

Urban planning - Living on the coast. People like to live near water. Real estate prices are an obvious testament to that. Studies have shown there is enough shoreline in the world to have all of the population of the world living within 1km of the ocean with lots left over.

We could collectively decide to only build cities near the ocean. Cities have no function other than it is a place where people congregate to be near other people and things that are "happening". Cities tend to be near rivers from the old days, when travelling by boat was the most efficient mode, but we don't need to do that anymore. We could consciously choose to focus our urban development to open shorelines. There are a few progressive countries out there that are trying to build smart, green cities in sustainable ways, but they are few and far between.

Why?

We don't like change. It seems like a crazy idea to pick up and move to another place in the world just to help out the planet, yet it is an idea that exists and is possible. Once again we just have to decide. If we valued the happiness of humans in general and not just ourselves or "our people" whomever you identify with, then we might just do it. Ideas like this are abundant.

Jobs - change the workplace - There are a ton of new ideas springing up about work life that are a departure from the old paradigms of competition. Workplaces whereby the boss treats people as human beings instead of a number are starting to multiply. Making people feel respected, valued and doing work that they are suited to do is growing in importance. Work is evolving and we should embrace it.

Happy City - in this book, Charles Montgomery cites studies that have shown people are happy when they live in an environment where they interact with other people. They realised that suburbia actually makes us feel disconnected from each other. People prefer to live in communities, where they can walk places and say hello to people. They want to have a mix of socioeconomic strata all intermingling - not gated communities and slums.

A neighbourhood that has rich people living right next to poor people has many benefits. As I discussed before, it creates a "safe" environment. This makes people more prone to self improvement and less prone to crime. It also gives people context. If you see only poverty, you have no idea what rich looks like in the real world, as opposed to TV and movies. Now you can see and touch it because you live next door to a millionaire. You may even say hello to him or her on the street. "Rich" is no longer an abstract concept, it is embodied by a real-live human being.

It works in the opposite direction too. If you only associate with other wealthy people, you have absolutely no real exposure to poverty, or to people who are struggling. You would only be comparing yourself to other rich people instead of having the opportunity to count your blessings everyday as you interact with people less fortunate than you.

I could go on and on. These are not my ideas, this is real data that has been collected by people who study this stuff for a living. Good urban planning is a very real and immediate solution for wealth disparity and human happiness.

I grew up in a small town in northern Alberta, Canada where everyone knew everyone. We all lived relatively close to each other. There was only one school for each level and we all attended class together, rich and poor. We played hockey together and chased the same girls. As young people, we really didn't even know who "Had Money" and who didn't. We were all just people. We all had to co-exist in spite of our differing economic circumstances. As we were in such close proximity, we dressed the same and attended most of the same social functions. Our parents all worked together and were friends. This environment didn't have the abstraction layer of "Gated Communities" or "bad neighbourhoods" to create artificial walls between us. Ask most people from small towns and they will usually tell you the same thing. Rich and poor can live together in harmony because it happens all the time. It is only in cites and overpopulated areas that socioeconomic status becomes a definitive set of strata. This is why many cities, such as Vancouver, Canada have started to make city bylaws that demand inclusion of affordable housing in any new urban developments. I love it.

ENVIRONMENTALISM- IS IT TOO IDEALISTIC?

Well, maybe, maybe not.

Environmentalism is definitely a component of a caring economy, and as such, should be respected as a trusted partner, not the gospel. We live on the earth and we should respect our home, but there is no need to go back to living in caves and picking berries to survive. There needs to be a partnership with the earth. The domination model has led us down the path of raping the earth for our own gain, without consideration for the consequences of our actions. Profit, being the name of the game, means MORE, and as long as the earth keeps giving, we will keep taking. This cannot work long-term.

Yet, we have advanced as a species enough that we can find a way to live in harmony with nature without going too far. We still need infrastructure, we still need homes and places to work and socialise. We still need to get from place to place, but it can all happen in a more sensible and cooperative manner.

Proper urban planning would ensure we could walk to most of the places we need to go instead of driving.

Proper public transportation system would ensure we use less resources and maximise the efficiency of transportation corridors.

Electric, self driving cars and ride sharing could eliminate the need for personal car ownership. I believe this is inevitable. This would make a huge environmental impact for the good guys. Most cars sit idle 90% of the time. If we all just called an automated car when we needed, it would free up the car to do other things. This would reduce the need for as many cars as there are. No more rush hour.

As more and more people work from home, the traditional commute to the office is less common and reduces the need for cars as well.

Mobile workforces and digital nomad lifestyles can even make huge cities less desirable. Minimalism and frugality will also contribute to cities being less of a draw. Traditionally people moved to cities for jobs. This is not going to be the case for much longer, as connectivity to the internet becomes more ubiquitous. People can work and be productive from anywhere.

We already have philosophies, technology, and workable systems to allow us to live in harmony with nature right now, and there is no longer any economic need to keep using resources at the rate we are consuming them. As more people wake up to these new ideas, the more we can collectively do what is right and best for our planet and our species. These are not unsolvable problems anymore. It only requires adoption now. Hopefully this book contributes to the spreading of the word.

WORLD GOVERNMENT

Countries - The concept of countries is actually starting to become a little dated. We are so used to it that we immediately cringe at the thought of eliminating them. Patriotism is considered a noble trait and treason is still one of the most contemptible crimes you can commit. Yet, I am merely trying to shake the cobwebs out of your brain and get you to see new possibilities as much as just see your existing beliefs and concepts for what they are.

To resurrect the spirit of John Lennon I ask you..

What if there were no countries? What if we just all lived on earth? Yes, immediately people ask who will be in charge? Where is our allegiance? Who's culture will rule?

These questions are a result of dominance thinking. We believe that someone needs to be in charge. Yes, that is true. Studies have shown that we function better when there is a clear hierarchy and we know who is in charge. I am absolutely not speaking about anarchy here. I am speaking about trying to reduce the "us vs. them" thinking that is propagated by nationalism. Hearing politicians talk about the "interests of our nation" is a little weird when you hear it as a person living outside of that particular nation.

We historically have believed that every nation should just take care of themselves, but that tends to create a competitive environment where there are haves and have nots, and conflicts arise over territory, trade, power and whatever reasons. Wars are not necessary any more. They are purely a power play between groups that are trying to maintain power over others or move economic objectives forward that serve the few, not the many.

I get it, nations make us feel "safe". It is just feudalism at a much larger scale. Our borders replace castle walls and our leaders replace the king. But the serfdom is still the same.

The world is not as dangerous a place as they might have you believe. Yet you are expected to salute the flag and put your national interests above that of all the other people of the earth. That just creates a monopoly type situation where eventually there is one winner and everyone else loses. We need to start thinking about humanity as a whole.

I find it hard to believe that there are people out there who's only intent is to attack and kill us because we are who we are. I find it hard to believe that there are groups of people who are plotting to destroy our way of life because they are just mean and spiteful, or believe that their way of life is so much better than ours that they feel fully justified in killing us all to make their point. This just isn't believable. Yet, that is what the concept of the nation state would have you believe. We believe that if we had no borders violent marauders would run amok and rape, kill and plunder at will. The fact is, the vast majority of people on the planet are quite content with their slice of the world and could care less about your particular way of life. In fact, I would suggest that the only "people" who want to attack and kill you, are those whom your particular "way of life" has been imposed upon. Nobody want to be oppressed. People don't start wars or commit acts of terrorism because it is fun. They do it out of desperation. They do it because they feel they have no other choice, due to some overbearing circumstance out of their control.

I believe that eliminating poverty through propagating a foundation of basic survival policies would enable people access to education. If we educate people, they are less likely to believe superstitious ideas that perpetuate holy wars, the oppression of women, or the inevitable return of a saviour who has one particular race/religion in its favour. They are less likely to commit inhuman acts in the name of religion because the critical thinking necessary to put religious teaching in context will have been gained through higher education.

LIFT THEM UP

I don't disagree with the capitalist notion of " a rising tide floats all boats" but I still would like to see a foundation for all the boats. A permanent body of water - to perpetuate the metaphor, so that at least everyone has a chance.

I have faith in people. I am constantly amazed at the innovations and progress made by people, not because they are paid to do so but because the human spirit will not be tamed. If everyone were taken care of, we would NOT sit on our couches all day and do nothing. We would continue to grow and strive. Strife is such a necessary part of life. We naturally seek it. It is in our nature. Sure, some people would not amount to much, and that is OK, at least they will not have the burden of survival to perhaps coax them into nefarious activities or self destruction. At worst, some folks might suffer an existential crisis as they need to find a new purpose. Survival is compelling as a purpose, but not very inspiring.

PEOPLE

Overpopulation is a very serious problem that we could do something about from a financial perspective. It is a bit of a chicken and egg situation. People tend to have a lot of children when they do not have access to education, birth-control and modern critical thinking. This tends to be in third world countries where they are already overpopulated. In modern countries, there is a very low, sometime a negative birthrate. Why? Because people are busy doing things. They have the time and resources to spend on themselves and feel they have choices. Women, especially in impoverished nations, are often not allowed access to education and birth control. They often have many children because they are dependant on a dominating male to take care of them and don't have the right to refuse their sexual advances. Sometimes it is more helpful to bear lots of children so the odds of at least one of them becoming successful and being able to care for the rest of the family are higher. I am not sure this is actually true, but that is the thinking.

If everyone had access to food, clothing and shelter, and perhaps education, we could lift these people out of ignorance and superstition and allow them to make decisions based on what is best for humanity, instead of from a state of desperation. Desperation tends to have a deleterious effect on morals and compassion, and when you live in a society that has too many people, there is no room for compassion, caring and even courtesy. It is every man for himself. Overpopulation does not promote cooperation, it creates competition of the most callous and uncaring nature. People stop being human and become objects, due to the sheer volume of them.

I believe that by providing a base level of sustenance, people will naturally have fewer babies, and the population of the earth will normalise itself so that it becomes sustainable and perhaps, cooperatively, we can ensure a good quality of life for everyone, at a minimum. There still needs to be equal parts of both competition and cooperation, as they both serve a purpose, but never allow either to take over.

People who are well feed, healthy and educated will be less inclined to make decisions that benefit only themselves.

TOP DOWN ECONOMICS

Does a rising tide floats all boats?

No, because fewer people control the money as time goes

on. Recycling wealth is part of the solution but it is only perpetuating the problem for longer. It is similar to urban planning, in that, if you build more roads to alleviate traffic congestion, you are just inviting more traffic , which creates more congestion. You will never be able to build enough roads. Economics is similar. There will never be enough money, because greed and inflation will eliminate all the gains. We have to fundamentally change the system. That is the only sustainable way we can move forward.

Utopia - No, but better. We can at least create a picture of what we seek. We need to have the courage to strive for a better world. As many success gurus say, it is not what you achieve that matters, it is who you become in the pursuit of it.

I agree.

As a society, if we try to make things better and we fail, that is OK. We will be better than we were before because we will have learned something. We will have figured out, at worst, how NOT to do things. We will, at best, figure out how to make more people happy and less people sad. We cannot sit and accept things as they are. They cannot continue this way, and we can all be a part of the solution. Tempered capitalism is a means to an end, not the ultimate end. We must constantly evolve our thinking and our behaviours if we are to survive as a species. Once again, the most adaptable survive.

We don't need to buy into a consumerist lifestyle. Everything costs money. Every thing is owned or claimed by someone, and you must pay to play. Basic survival should be free.

Nestle tried to own all of the fresh water. This is capitalism run amok. It was not allowed to happen, but what type of mindset needs to exist to even contemplate such a thing? Would having a monopoly on all the fresh water in the world benefit us all? I don't think so.

Jordan Peterson suggested that society works best when approached with a biblical metaphor of equal hands of justice and mercy.

If there is too much mercy then the people run amok and this creates pathology.

If there is too much justice (ie. discipline) then that equals pathology as well. The two hands need to be tempered by each other . Capitalism needs the same treatment - you cannot have too much hippy-dippy socialism yet you can't be too far in the other direction either - both create an unsustainable de-humanising society of either aimless hunters and gatherers or one monopoly winner ruling the impoverished masses.

So we come to a logical conclusion; That we need to reimagine the relationship between the two ideologies of Capitalism and Socialism. We need to embrace the value inherent in both systems and work together as a partnership. Just like Ms. Eisler suggested, we need to have the masculine tendencies of Capitalism and the feminine qualities of Socialism form a partnership whereby each brings its own strengths to the table when the situation calls for it and steps aside when the other path is called for.

It is a model whereby we contextualise each "ism" and realise that each of these two apparently diametrically opposed ideologies are actually useful when put into the proper framework. Just like the vision the modern day feminists have put forth, where men and women and their natural tendencies are valued equally and respected for what they bring to the shared experience we all are a part of, these two schools of thought can co-exist if we just learn to temper them with limits and try to see how we can use them for the benefit of all. Hard woking, creative and productive people MUST be compensated fairly for their efforts and our society cannot function without them. We need competition and a fair meritocracy to drive innovation, and create a better world. We also need to ensure everyone has the opportunity to pursue these things if they wish. We cannot let unabated greed and domination behaviours drive those who are less equipped to play into oblivion. We need to take care of people. We need to take care of our planet. We need to value the things that sustain us and respect and honour our personal differences. We are all unique individuals with our own special contribution to make in the world. If we are struggling to survive or are surrounded by poverty, crime and ignorance, we are facing a tough situation that really isn't conducive to being our best selves, or contributing to society in a meaningful way.

We can do this. It will be hard. It might seem improbable in a world where everyone is divided and judgemental and unwilling to carefully consider our interconnectedness. We created our sociological structures and now we believe they exist outside of ourselves and are immutable.

We have forgotten our own personal power and sovereignty. We must sit down with our smartest people and construct a world where everyone is taken care of, the earth is taken care of, and society can still be incentivised to create and progress.

Changes like converting to renewable energy or becoming a paperless world are great, but they even require capital. What I am talking about only requires a change of mindset.

Yes, as you change the world, there are some people who stand to lose some ground. The super-rich might just have to settle for being only "*very*" rich. But perhaps the super-poor could be less poor and have a liveable existence. They could be housed, and fed and clothed and educated, with access to healthcare. With these minimum standards in place, we could set the stage for a world where we all are inspired to maximise our potential. Perhaps we could even learn to get along with each other.

I believe a minimum standard of living policy would drastically reduce crime, addiction, truancy, health care costs and the need for massive, expensive incarceration and judicial/police systems. People would perhaps trade a sense of desperation for a sense of purpose. Maybe they would be able to find a longing in themselves to see what they might be capable of. Perhaps without having to worry about how they are going to feed themselves people could be thinking about how they can become more than they were yesterday. The elevation of the self and the individual is a necessary step in the collective evolution of society as a whole. Societies are built upon principles first, not economies. When you come to a first world nation from a third world nation, it is incumbent upon you to learn that truth. Our society does not exist because the streets are paved with gold, our peaceful, democratic society exists because the people who built it had ideals. The ideals were freedom from tyranny, equal opportunity for all and that hard working, productive people should have their just rewards.

The time has come for us to wake up and see that we are ready to find that happy medium. We have enough information, data and history to realise that the way forward is to take the best of what we have learned and forge a new path that includes capitalism, socialism, feminism, patriarchy, and all the other "isms" you can think of and find out what they were trying to achieve. Study them and construct a new model of the world that works for everyone. It is a massive undertaking and it would be forced to contend with a great many rigid ideals and closed minds. It would be bumping up against people and societies that feel they have something to lose by changing.

The objective here is to just bring awareness. I am not

about to change the world. I just want to explore the ideas. We can bring these ideas into reality slowly over time. We have progressed so much in the last century. Even in my lifetime I have seen dramatic changes in opinions and behaviours to previously oppressed people. Attitudes about things like race, religion, gender, sexual orientation, and socioeconomic status have all made huge strides forwards. I admit they still have more work to be done, but the awareness in the collective consciousness that we need to wake up is not limited to just these issues. The underlying ideas do not exist in a bubble. I derived a lot of the ideas in this book from books and media that were addressing other topics.

The "post-modernist" culture seem to be a catalyst for change, even though their stance is far too "left" to be realistic, yet the momentum they created is a beautiful force for correction. The world works best when there is harmony. Balance between the two sides of our nature. We can support and lean on each other, and respect and value each other for our contributions, whether liberal or conservative, republican or democrat, Christian, Jew or Muslim. We must concede to the "middle ground" and realise the centre is where the real action is. Right wing, left wing, it's all a part of the process. Psychology vs sociology. Both disciplines have value and help us to understand our world. Both are necessary, yet neither one should be the guiding light to salvation. We must have both. We must respect the contributions of both disciplines. We need to get our own act together as individuals and clean up our collective backyard too. One does not precede the other.

If we are to survive, and perhaps even thrive and grow as a species we need to find that middle ground. We need to face the future together, man and woman, hand in hand, as a team. We need to bring our best selves to the challenges we face individually and collectively, so we need to set ourselves up for success by ensuring that we give everyone a chance to be that "best self" and be a part of the solution. We have the potential to be amazing creatures and we are capable of greatness. We are also far too capable of evil and destruction. We need to choose. I think when we can spread awareness of higher ideals and new concepts it helps to reduce the propensity for selfishness and "service to self" behaviours.

We will always need to contend with our human imperfections. We are emotional, and irrational, and we tend towards self-preservation in a crisis over the general good, but we can take steps towards the ideal, and fill our minds with new ideas. We must try to wake up to the ways that we think and act that just don't make sense anymore.

Yes, continue your fight. We still need to ensure all people are truly respected, valued and given equal opportunities. We still need to push further towards partnership and cooperation from the domination and competition paradigm. Partnership is not the opposite of domination it is the middle. Submission is the opposite of domination and nobody wants that.

EPILOGUE

I guess what this all comes down to is balance. The balance between two forces that should be in partnership. The male and the female. The yin and the yang. The universe seems to be made from a symbolic symbiosis between the hand of justice and the hand of mercy. So many aspects of our existence are best explained by this apparent good cop bad cop scenario, and many sociological and psychological tenets are built upon a healthy dose of each. Neither mindset was ever meant to rule. A healthy society, just like a healthy psyche, is dependent upon embracing both aspects of ourselves and using each when necessary.

We are collectively immersed in a sea of sociological constructs that we have given so much power to, they have taken on a life of their own. We are willing to fight and die for king, country, church, and state without realising that these things are just ideas, they are not real things. We made them up. We absolutely need them in our lives to give our world a semblance of order and purpose.

Yes, we tend to be happier when we feel like we belong to something bigger than ourselves, but we need to, at least, be aware that the "bigger things" that we pledge ourselves to are not always immutable or absolute. They are constructs that we designed and are free to change if they no longer serve us. Ultimately the sovereignty of the individual cannot always be subordinate to the sociological construct or vice-versa.

In this sense, we have created a construct called "Economics" or "Capitalism" that we blindly adhere to and give our lives to serving, yet it is inherently broken. It serves the few and leaves the rest to perish. We need to correct that system and redesign it to service the greater good. We need to find out what a "Caring economy" looks like and try to modify our perceptions and behaviours to serve that end. We can no longer believe that the only purpose of a business is to make money or a corporation is solely beholden to its shareholders, like Milton Friedman put forth through his writings .

Even the Harvard Business Review (HBR) has questioned whether capitalism has lost its way. This questioning of the status quo is by no means arguing that we need to go crazy and adhere to some new "ism" that turns the current system on its head. We need to evolve. We don't want to throw away the baby with the bathwater, and do away with capitalism altogether. We want to take what is a good idea and make it great. The problem with Capitalism and socialism and communism etc is the context in which it exists. If any of these systems gets put into place in the context of a society that is mired in patriarchal domination or religious fundamentalism, it is most likely doomed to fail, because the undercurrent of control and competition will cause the system to become corrupt and self serving to those in control.

Inversely if we try to implement these systems in a hippy-dippy way where we assume everyone is loved and no one should have more than anyone else we are going against basic human nature and we will crash and burn in spectacular fashion.

We need to truly create a system where partnership and mutual respect is paramount, where we appreciate the value that competition *and* cooperation each bring to the playing field. We need to find a way to be able to see the point of view of the other. Men and women, when given equal rights, opportunities and permissions, make the world a better place because they are different. We need to embrace both approaches to life in order to maintain the balance.

I have used the terms Partnership and Cooperation interchangeably throughout this work for ease of use yet I realise they are slightly different concepts. I am always keenly aware that competition and domination are very different as well. Please do not be thrown off by this, I am just bringing to light our general biases and the writing would be cumbersome if I was always making a four-sided argument instead of two. I feel like you get my drift.

Fascism was evil because it only appreciated the hand of justice and that is why it ultimately failed. Communism was evil because it only appreciated the hand of mercy and crushed the spirit of the ambitious and innovative. Neither mindset will work because we are a population equally divided into those that cooperate and those that compete. We cannot succeed unless we use both faculties in equal measure. We must respect and honour the contributions of the past and move forward into the future with new ideas.

I have mentioned some new ideas in this book that are alternatives to our traditional capitalist system in order to break the mould. I believe that capitalism is responsible for great progress and has contributed to general prosperity and overall human well-being in immeasurable ways. It has lifted us out of hardship and created opportunities that were never imagined even a century ago. We owe a debt of gratitude to it's works, and it deserves to be admired.

But it is not perfect, and it is not beyond reproach. We

invented capitalism and we should not be so enamoured by its grandeur that we are afraid to consider it a "work in progress", for it still is. It has a few rough edges that need a little tweaking to get "just right". We can make it even greater than it already is. We can make it universally appealing and beneficial. Imagine if we made it so appealing that other "isms" couldn't help themselves but to adopt its practice.

It is possible. We have a much better handle on where the issues lay, and we are inexorably moving towards a more egalitarian society everyday. We are learning through trial and error that a patriarchal approach to any society makes it less effective than if we build that society on a foundation of partnership between our two natures.

ACKNOWLEDGMENTS

This book would not be possible without the love, encouragement and support of my family. I would have no purpose if it were not for you.

ALSO BY PERI SCOTT

BYOB : Be Your Own Bank

Invest In Yourself

What I Wish I Knew About Money

PERI SCOTT

Author, Entrepreneur, Father, Musician

Peri Scott is an evangelist for financial literacy and human potential. He believes we live in the best time in history to take advantage of opportunities to grow and prosper.

Peri lives in Canada with his family and loves hockey.

This is Peri's fourth book.

Visit Peri at:

www.beyourownbank.ca

www.periscott.com

www.ingramcontent.com/pod-product-compliance
Ingram Content Group UK Ltd.
Pitfield, Milton Keynes, MK11 3LW, UK
UKHW020422250726
13967UKWH00007B/2778